To order copies
Amazon.com
Barnes and Noble.com
Createspace.com/3656573

No Excuses – A Guide Out of Poverty

Copyright 2004 by Elie V. Parker

<u>Dedication</u>

The book is dedicated to the millions of Black and poor people struggling to escape poverty. It is the goal of this book to give direction and guidance out of poverty and suffering and into hope and prosperity.

Title of Book

"No Excuses - A Guide Out of Poverty"
By Elie V. Parker

Contents

Chapters: Page

Preface

The purposes of this book is to show how Black people or anyone who is poor can escape poverty and achieve prosperity by building businesses, improving education, eating healthy, planning families, looking and acting professional, voting and avoiding vices such as, alcohol, drugs and tobacco products. The book is based on the conviction that Blacks should not expect White people or the government to provide for them. The book emphasizes the need for Blacks to embrace the concept of self-determination and by pooling resources, build their way out of poverty. I plans to use this book as a platform to not only talk about what needs to be done but to work in the Black communities to ensure that Blacks accomplish what needs to be done.

This book is different from other books on Black poverty because it asks for no government or corporate help. The book asserts two things. One, only Blacks can save Blacks and that Blacks can be saved by building Black businesses that produce jobs and create wealth. Two, Blacks need to refrain from those activities that take wealth away like poor eating habits, unplanned pregnancies and illegal drugs.

This book will show how Blacks and the poor can move out of poverty. This will be accomplished by identifying a series of steps that each individual can take on their own and collectively with others.

My educational background is a Bachelor of Science in Business Administration in Accounting and Economics from Youngstown State University in Youngstown, Ohio and a Master's Degree in Business Administration in Finance from DePaul University in Chicago, Illinois.

I served in the United States Army from 1968 to 1970, which included a year in South Vietnam. I received the National Defense Service Medal, Vietnam Service Medal w/ 4 Bronze Service Stars, Republic of Vietnam Campaign Medal and the Army Commendation Medal.

I worked for United Airlines for 31 years in various accounting, financial and auditing functions.

I have seen the world from both sides having worked for United Airlines in management and I worked for Youngstown Sheet and Tube as a general laborer and a union member.

I believe that my experience, education and goal to end poverty make me uniquely qualified to present this book as my contribution to the world's effort to make the planet a better place for everyone.

Elie V. Parker

E–mail: evp324@sbcglobal.net

Chapter 1 – Black History

> **For most of our history, we have depended on the good will of others to sustain us.**

Black Dependency

For over a century, no government program or charitable contribution has been able to end poverty in the Black community. Even with all of the billions spent over the years, we still find today that over 25 percent of the Black race lives in poverty. Also many of those who are working are doing jobs far below their ability.

For most of our history, we have depended on the good will of others to sustain us. Our jobs, our education and our housing are for the most part, created, taught, built and controlled by groups other than us.

Blacks own no fortune 500 companies, no large national banks and own few companies with a workforce greater than 100 employees. As a result, we employ few Blacks in the community, build few homes, and control few of the financial decisions that affect our lives.

We are at the mercy of others and our poor financial status reflects that.

Affirmative Action

At one time, it was thought that affirmative action could end Black poverty but resistance to the affirmative action programs have made them ineffective and limited in results. Although, affirmation action has been around for over 30 years, of the top 500 US corporations about 1% has a Black CEO. Also, Black unemployment is still twice the rate of White unemployment. Because of a lack of jobs, young Black males are 5 times more likely to be sent to one of America's prisons than young White men. Because there has been little educational advancement in the public school system, Black kids today are not speaking or reading any better than they were ten years ago. The high unemployment rate, high incarceration rate and low education levels have kept the poverty rate in the Black community consistently between 23 to 30 percent whether the economy is good or bad.

Blacks Need a Business Strategy

As mentioned above, up to this point, Blacks have depended on programs like affirmative action to escape poverty. These programs have not been effective enough to end poverty in the Black community. Blacks need a new strategy and I suggest a business strategy. If Blacks build their own schools and business, they would not have to depend on affirmative action to do it for them. Resources in the Black community should be pooled and committed to building an economy that can end poverty and end the policy of begging for a few crumbs from the affirmative action table. It is time for Blacks to step onto the light of self-determination and build their way out of poverty. If Blacks spend less time depending on others and more time depending on themselves, they can take their place in the advancement of the human race. **It is more effective to build than it is to beg.**

The reasons we must build the Black economy are as follows:

1) The Black unemployment rate today is worse than it was thirty years ago.

2) Black unemployment is nearly twice the national average.

3) Net worth of Blacks is 10% of a White persons net worth.

4) Businesses owned by Blacks are small and employ few Black workers.

5) 32% of the Black male population has a police record.

6) 86% of today's young Black women are single when they have their first child.

7) 70 % of Black children are born out of wedlock. Many are locked into poverty for the rest of their lives.

8) 50 % of Black children in single-mother families in 2008 live in poverty.

9) The reading scores of Black children are some of the lowest in the nation.

Other groups, who found themselves in poverty, have escaped by pooling their resources and building their way out. Today, they own the fortune 500 companies.

Blacks need to take control of their destiny. This can be accomplished by controlling the Black environment. This book will describe the Black environment and advise on how it can be developed to end poverty in the Black community.

Summary of Chapter 1 – Black History

1) Today 25% of the Black race lives in poverty.
2) Blacks create few jobs, own few major educational institutions and build few homes.
3) Blacks own no fortune 500 companies.
4) Less than 1% of the top 500 US corporations have Black CEOs.
5) Black unemployment is nearly twice the rate of White unemployment.
6) Due to the lack of jobs, young Black males are 5 times more likely to be sent to one of America's prisons than young White men.
7) Because there has been little educational advancement in the public school system, Black kids today are not speaking or reading any better than they were ten years ago.
8) The high unemployment rate, high incarceration rate and low education levels have kept the poverty rate in the Black community consistently between 23 to 30 percent whether the economy is good or bad.
9) Affirmative Action has failed.
10) Blacks need a business strategy.

Chapter 2 - Civil Rights to Corporate Giants

Blacks need to move from customers to owners from borrowers to lenders, from the recipient of services to the provider of services.

The Civil Rights Battle has been won

Congratulation, the battle for civil rights has been won. Most Blacks can vote, Blacks can eat in most restaurants or at least the ones you would want to eat at and some of the best hotels in the country have thrown their doors open to people of a darker skin.

The civil right groups (NAACP, Push, National Urban League) and countless other civil rights organizations who marshaled their collective energies to fight racism can now turn their attention to the next battle field, an economic battle field.

The new battlefield will require different tactics and skills. The battle must now move from trying to get serviced in the restaurants to owning the restaurant that serves the meals. Where as in the past, Blacks could not get into the hotels; the new battle is to raise the money to finance the building and ownership of the hotels. Blacks need to move from customers to owners from borrowers to lenders, from the recipient of services to the provider of services.

National and Global Structures are Already in Place

The civil right organizations already have national structures and global reach. Many of these groups like the NAACP have branch offices in every part of the country. Many of their officers have contacts in many of the nations of the world.

Skills Needed for the New Battle

Bankers, accountants, engineers, teachers, scientist, salespersons, marketers, computer analyst, lawyers and all the other skills needed to build an economy will be required.

Conversion From Non-profit to Profit

The civil rights groups must convert from nonprofit organizations to profit making enterprises. Growth is only possible by making a profit. May of the civil rights groups have a tax-exempt status because they are non-profit. Unfortunately, the tax-exempt status only guarantees that you will stay poor because if you make a profit the exemption is taken away. There are much better ways to minimize your taxes than a tax-exempt status and at the same time earn billions of dollars that can be invested in Black companies and corporations that produce jobs and hope in the Black community. By given up the tax-exempt status and the few tax dollars saved, the Black community can make billions in profits and reinvest the money in the poor neighborhoods that desperately need help. Currently, the tax-exempt status will not allow you to make enough money to take care of yourself. Also, when the Black civil rights groups turn in their tax-exempt status, it will be a signal to the world that Black people can make it on their own and that they do not need a government handout.

Summary - Chapter 2 - Civil Rights to Corporate Giants

1) The battle for civil rights has been won.
2) The battle for business dominance has just begun.
3) Non-profit tax-exempts companies are designed to keep you poor and must be replaced with companies that can grow, earn profits, create jobs and end poverty in the Black communities.

Chapter 3 – Black Business

For Every Consumer need there is a Business Solution

Blacks must Build Economic Power

Blacks are going nowhere in America without economic power. Economic power comes from business. Blacks need to go into every type of business venture there is, from banking to manufacturing to food production and distribution to insurance to education. They need to be in every aspect of trade and commerce because through business activities jobs are created, basic needs of food and shelter are fulfilled and growth and self-advancement is possible.

The African American community has plenty of money to build an economy large and strong enough to end poverty. Billions of dollars pass through the Black community each year. They only have to pool and channel these funds into income producing ventures. In other words, money needs to be turned over several times in the community in order for it to work more efficiently for the community. Currently, in most Black communities, there are not enough Black owned businesses to turn the dollar over enough times to generate the volume of jobs needed to end the high unemployment in the community. Contributing to this problem is the fact that the education system in the Black community is not effective enough to provide the skill level needed to build modern progressive businesses. Most Black businesses are the mom and pop type with small inventories and staff and offering the same level and quality of service they offered twenty years ago. Even when great changes have occurred in the business world outside of the Black communities, little has changed in the Black communities. For example, take a look at the banking industry. In 1998, the total staff of the top 25 Black banks in the United States was 2,030. In 2003 that number was 2,051, a net growth of 21 employees over a six-year period or an increase of 3.5 employees per year. To make matters worse, this was one of the greatest economic growth periods in US history. In 2009 the total number of employees in the top 25 Black banks was 2,003 or 48 less than year 2003, see

Figure 3.1 below. Actually, the number of employees in Black banks has barely moved in 30 years which is hardly the growth engine needed to fuel economic growth.

By comparison, in 2011 one White controlled bank, JP Morgan Chase & Co. had 240,000 employees in over 50 countries providing services from loans, investments, money management and insurance. With their size, they have the ability to create markets, finance domestic and international projects, influence governments and hire enough employees to maintain full or nearly full employment in their communities. That is the difference between Black companies and White companies. White companies understand the principles of economy of scale, which is; **the larger your company is the more you can influence the outcome of your business.**

Black owned, One United Bank has made a move to grow by acquiring and combining four banks; Family Saving Bank FSB Founders, National Bank of Los Angeles, Peoples National Bank of Commerce and Boston Bank of Commerce. More Black companies should review this type of growth model.

Figure 3.1

Black Bank Staffing 1998-2009

By Assets	Company	Location	Year Started	Staff 1998	Staff 2003	Staff 2009	Change 1998 - 2009
1	Carver Federal Saving Bank	New York, NY	1948	N/A	110	150	
2	Urban Trust Bank	Lake Mary, FL	1963	N/A	N/A	191	
3	One United Bank	Boston, MA	1982	N/A	143	112	
4	Broadway Federal Bank	Los Angeles, CA	1946	51	57	88	37
5	City National Bank of New Jersey	Newark, NJ	1973	63	90	104	41
6	Liberty Bank & Trust Co.	New Orleans, LA	1972	135	145	141	6
7	Citizens Bancshares	Atlanta, GA	1921	N/A	N/A	134	
8	Seaway National Bank of Chicago	Chicago, IL	1965	260	264	183	-77
9	Industrial Bank N.A.	Washington, DC	1934	159	170	137	-22
10	Capital City Bank & Trust Company	Atlanta, GA	1994	N/A	60	85	
11	The Harbor Bank of Maryland	Baltimore, MD	1982	71	80	77	6

Figure 3.1 Part II

Black Bank Staffing 1998-2009

By Assets	Company	Location	Year Started	Staff 1998	Staff 2003	Staff 2009	Change 1998 - 2009
12	Mechanics & Farmers Bank	Durham, NC	1908	78	93	74	-4
13	Legacy Bank	Milwaukee, WI	1999	N/A	22	40	
14	First Independence National Bank of Detroit	Detroit, MI	1970	70	60	82	12
15	Independence Federal Savings Bank	Washington, DC	1968	71	75	46	-25
16	Illinois Service Federal S&L Association	Chicago, IL	1934	45	50	46	1
17	Tri-State Bank of Memphis	Memphis, TN	1946	70	71	63	-7
18	Highland Community Bank	Chicago, IL	1970	120	76	39	-81
19	North Milwaukee State Bank	Milwaukee, WI	1971	N/A	N/A	23	
20	South Carolina Community Bank	Columbia, SC	1999	N/A	N/A	42	
21	Citizen Saving Bank & Trust	Nashville, TN	1904	N/A	N/A	23	

Figure 3.1 Part III

Black Bank Staffing 1998-2009

By Assets	Company	Location	Year Started	Staff 1998	Staff 2003	Staff 2009	Change 1998 - 2009
22	Advance Bank	Baltimore, MD	19577	N/A	N/A	35	
23	First Tuskegee Bank	Tuskegee, AL	1894	38	35	31	-7
24	Commonwealth National Bank	Mobile, AL	1976	N/A	N/A	30	
25	United Bank of Philadelphia	Philadelphia, PA	1992	80	50	27	-53

Chart source: Black Enterprise June 1998, June 2003 and June 2010 issue.

Mom and Pop Shop must Consolidate

For years, I went to my local Black barber for a haircut. It was a social gathering as much as a place to get a hair cut. There was loud talk, a pool table to grab a game before your cut and occasionally the neighborhood entrepreneur would show up with jewels, radios, or even a ham that happen to have fallen off a nearby truck or train. These barber shops never changed. They were usually in unclean and often unsafe locations. The hair products used were decades behind current technology. The haircut I got was not the one I asked for but the one the barber felt like giving me. The barber seemed more interested in the pool game than in what type of haircut I wanted. Customer is always right or at least most of the time did not seem to apply. Also, the price for a cut increased without any regard to supply and demand. These problems were bad enough but the biggest hurdle was the time it took to get a haircut. It took from two to five hours to get a haircut. Any person trying to get an education, run a business or support a family does not have the time to take a day or a half of a day off to get a haircut. I endured this treatment for years until one day a Supercuts barbershop opened near me. They had clean shops in safe locations. Their products were current. They gave me the cut I requested. Their price was half the price of my previous barber and they were fast. Twenty to thirty minutes and my haircut was done.

Supercuts took a seemly-dispersed business and consolidated it under one management. By doing this, they were able to establish universal quality standards, negotiate discounted leases and products, advertise locally and nationally which increased their customer base which enables them to drop prices and increase their services.

The Black mom and pop shops need to become the Super Cuts of the future. Whether the service is hair salon, car repair, wedding planning, catering, selling groceries, lending money, building homes, insuring property and lives, the larger you are the better service or product you can provide at the lowest possible cost.

Build Them Large

Large companies and corporation is where the power and the future can be found. Through the economy of scale, customers can be found through national and international advertising. Funding for growth and expansion can be achieved by developing products and services that meet the needs of large groups of people in domestic and international markets.

The consolidation of the mom and pop stores in the Black community has kind of started. Small shops have met and formed associations. Associations can bring together expertise, contacts and money. The next step should be for these associations to form large companies and corporations.

Build Professional Businesses

A Jewish fellow once told me that the reason there were so many Jewish doctors and lawyers is because the major corporations would not hire Jews to work in their companies. The Jews had to start their own companies and professions in order to have a job. I think the same is true for Blacks. Only one percent of the top corporate officials are Black. If Blacks want the top jobs or professions, they will have to build them. Blacks need to start their own companies and professions. Also, becoming a doctor, lawyer, dentist, CPAs or one of the other professional occupations is a great way to make a living and provide a service to your community. These careers can bring status and wealth to the Black community just like they did to the Jewish community.

Support groups need to be established to identify promising students who can qualify for these professional positions and they should be financed, encouraged and supported through the entire process. Student's support should start on the first day of school to the first patient or client.

Support groups or sponsors can be the student's church, family members, neighborhood block club, or any other group of people that want to see an end to poverty in the community. Family reunions would be a good place to build a support group. Each family could work to have at least one doctor or lawyer in the family. In turn, the family lawyer or doctor can provide services to the family, which enriches the whole family and the community.

Avoid Building the wrong type of Business

The Black community needs companies that will make a positive contribution to their health, education, and welfare. For decades, the African American communities have been a dumping ground for products and services that are over priced, counterproductive, hazardous and illegal. For example, take the booze industry. The poor Black communities are festooned with liquor advertising signs. These signs encourage Blacks to drink more even though; drinking has brought a high level of spouse and child abuse, job loss, family disintegration and crime to the community. In some communities, there are more liquor stores than any other type of businesses. This is not the right type of business you want in your community. This type of business will bring more harm than good. Other types of businesses harmful to the Black communities are the McDonalds, Burger Kings, Pizza Hut, Kentucky Fried Chicken and other fast food restaurants. Their products are hazardous to your health with their high content of sodium, fat, cholesterol and calories. When these restaurants are present it is a sure signal that you have entered a Black or poor community. Their products are peddled to the less informed. For every dollar they might bring into the community, they will cost the community tens of thousands of dollars in health related illness caused by their products.

The Trend for 2003 is not good

The top 100 Black Enterprise Industrial companies from 1998 to 2003 increased employment from 48,005 to 75,020 or a gain of 27,015. Of the top ten companies, see Figure 3.2 below, the two top companies was Burger King and Wendy's. Hamburger and pizza companies were the fastest growing employer in 2003. These are low paying, low skilled companies. Also they sell a product high in fat, cholesterol, and sodium, which are ingredients known to contribute to the high rate of diabetes, strokes and heart attacks in the Black communities. These are not the right type of companies you want to encourage in the community. They bring obesity, illness and death to the Black family.

Figure 3.2

Top 10 B.E. Industrial Companies with the most staff from 1998 to 2003

B.E. Industrial companies with the most Staff:	Product or Service	1998	2003	Net Gain
The La-Van Hawkins Food Group	Burger King	2643	7133	4490
Manna Inc	Wendy's Hamburgers	N/A	6000	6000
MV Transportation Inc	Fixed route & transit service	N/A	4186	4186
Barden Cos. Inc.	Casino gaming, real estate	1600	4050	2450
The Bartech Group Inc.	Professional Staffing	1640	3800	2160
V&J Holding Cos. Inc.	Burger King & Pizza Hut	2400	3500	1100
Omniplex	Security, investigations, inventory loss prevention	N/A	3000	3000
Thompson Hospitality	Contract food service restaurants	1500	2500	1000
Exemplar Manufacturing Co.	Metal fasteners & assemblies	140	2302	2162
RLLW Inc.	Pizza Hut & airport retail	N/A	2200	2200
Total		9923	38671	28748

Source: Black Enterprise Magazine

Lessons Learned

By 2009 the top 10 B.E. Industrial companies in 1998 have not done well. Of the top ten, three have gone out of business each with a teaching moment. La-Van Hawkins of The La-Van Hawkins Food Group was convicted of fraud and perjury and failure to pay federal taxes. In 2003 Exemplar Manufacturing Co. filed for Chapter 11 bankruptcy after General Motors and Ford pulled their contracts. RLLW Inc. failed to pay their workers compensation insurance and closed in May 2004

The lessons learned is run an honest business, pay your taxes on time and do not depend on a few customers to keep your company in business.

The building blocks of a sustainable business are:
Honest, Integrity and Quality Goods and Services.

The Trend for 2009 is also not good

As in 2003 the 2009 outlook for advancing progressive Black businesses is disappointing. Like 2003 some of the fastest growing Black businesses are fast food restaurants servicing food high in fat, cholesterol, and sodium, see figure 3.3 below.

A positive on Figure 3.3 was MV Transportation which added employees. Also Black Enterprise did report that the number one B.E Industrial/Service Company in revenue 2009 was a tech company called World Wide Technology with $ 2.2 billion in revenue.

Figure 3.3

Top 10 B.E. Industrial Companies with Most Staff from 1998 to 2009

B.E. Industrial companies with the most Staff:	Product or Service	1998	2003	2009	Net Gain
The La-Van Hawkins Food Group *	Burger King	2643	7133	N/A	-7133
Manna Inc *	Wendy's Hamburgers	N/A	6000	11250	5250
MV Transportation Inc	Fixed route & Para transit service	N/A	4186	12880	8694
Barden Cos. Inc.	Casino gaming, real estate	1600	4050	3350	-700
The Bartech Group Inc.	Professional Staffing	1640	3800	200	-3600
V&J Holding Cos. Inc. *	Burger King & Pizza Hut	2400	3500	4500	1000
Omniplex	Security, investigations, inventory loss prevention	N/A	3000	1075	-1925
Thompson Hospitality	Contract food service restaurants	1500	2500	3300	800
Exemplar Manufacturing Co.	Metal fasteners & assemblies	140	2302	N/A	-2302
RLLW Inc. *	Pizza Hut & airport retail	N/A	2200	N/A	-2200
Total		9923	38671	36555	-2116

Source: Black Enterprise Magazine

Summary of Chapter 3 – Black Business

Build Baby Build.

1) Build large companies and corporations.
2) Build all types of business and provide all types of services.
3) Build professionals like doctors, lawyers and CPA's.
4) Produce services and products for large groups in domestic and international markets. Provide what is needed and wanted, at a competitive price.
5) Make your customer number one and never forget that your customer is number one.
6) Update. Update. Update. Remember the world (your customer) is always changing.
7) Be true to your community. Bring to them products that will make a positive contribution to their lives.
8) **Blacks need to build businesses that are honest, have integrity and produce quality goods and services.**

Chapter 4 – Employment and Unemployment:

Black unemployment rates are nearly twice the national average and have been for over the last thirty years.

Black Unemployment

Black unemployment, which has been as high as 15.7% is a depression level range. It is usually more than twice the national rate in good times or bad. Black unemployment over at least the last 30 years, has never been less than the national average, always more, see below (Figure 4.2) titled 'Unemployment by Race for the Last 30 Years'. The old saying that Blacks are the last hired and first fired is as true today as it was fifty years ago and will probably be fifty years from now unless Blacks change the work ownership relationship.

As mentioned in the business chapter, there are few Black businesses around to hire and retain Black people. When times get rough in any business, the last to go are the employees that are part of the old buddy system. The old buddy system is made up of the top managers of a company, their relatives, golf buddies, church members, luncheon crowd and other groups that make up the core of a company. Because America is segregated by race, in White companies, few Blacks are in these core groups and are therefore the first to go and the last to be hired. In order for Blacks to be the first hired and the last fired, they will have to own the companies they work for. By owning the company, Blacks can create their own old buddy system and avail themselves of the millions of jobs that are based on who you know rather that what you know.

Based on statistics from the U.S. Department of Labor, Figure 4.1 below, the national unemployment rate was 9.0% as of January 2011. The jobless rate by race is as follows:

1) Blacks (15.7 percent).
2) Whites (8.0 percent).
3) Hispanics (11.9 percent).
4) Asians (6.9 percent).

Figure 4.1

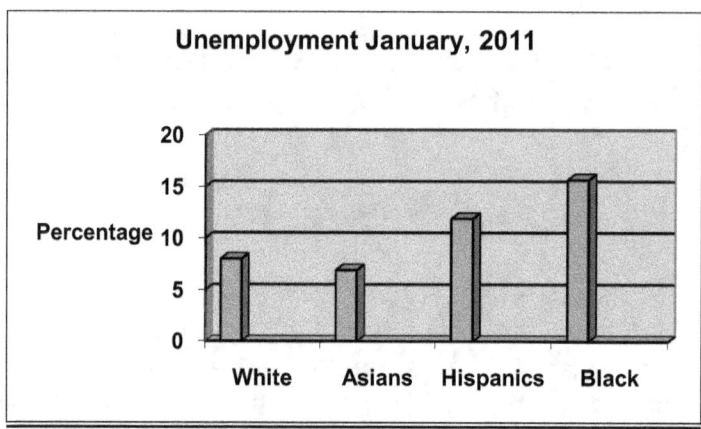

Over the last thirty eight years Black unemployment has worsen. In 1973, Black unemployment was 9 percent. By 2011 it had gone up to 15.7 percent or nearly twice the percentage for Whites and nearly twice the national average. In short, Blacks are worse off today than they were thirty eight years ago, see (Figure 4.2) below.

Figure 4.2

Unemployment By Race for the last 30 Years

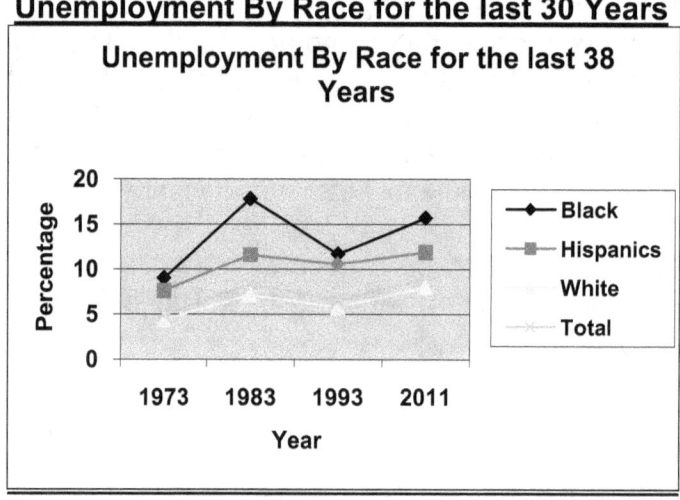

Source: US Department of Labor

Blacks must Build their Community from the Ground Up

What can a Black person do to end the high unemployment rate? Well almost everything. Life-styles must change, education must be enhanced and companies must be built. Jobs must be trained for and acquired. In the appendix is a list of some of the better paying jobs. Like any good job, they are competitive and require training and /or degrees. Good communication skills are a must and there is no room for Ebonics. These are jobs that are needed today and tomorrow.

Skilled Jobs are in

Unskilled jobs are out, skilled jobs are in and it has been that way for the last 30 years. The wage rate for jobs in the Third World or outside of the country are 90 to 95 percent less than in the United States. There is no way the wage rate for low skilled workers in America can compete with the low skilled workers' wage rate in less developed countries. Also, no amount of government regulations, tariffs or border guards can keep the impact of low wageworkers out of the United States. If corporate America cannot bring the low wageworkers into the United States, they will move the work out of the USA to the low wageworkers. The structure of capitalism requires that this be done. Corporation must seek the lows cost of labor and material in order for them to remain competitive and maximize profits and stockholders' return on investment. In addition, although, recent history shows that low skilled jobs are being transferred out of the United States, present trends also point out that the higher skilled jobs are also being transferred out of the country. Programmers, system analyst and other jobs in the technical fields are finding workers in poorer countries with educated populations such as India, China, Korea, and Eastern Europe. Job competition is becoming a globe issue. Not only must you prepare to compete with the person around the corner but also the person around the world.

Best and Only Job

The job you want is one that only you can do. Keep in mind that if someone else can do your job, than you can be replaced. If a country has 1000 doctors and it needs 2000, then your job is fairly safe. Or if you have the only degree in metallurgy and that skill is needed, the likelihood of you being unemployed is next to zero.

If others are doing similar work as you are, you can still separate yourself from the others. For example, a company may have many accountants but you can separate yourself from the other accountants by acquiring additional education such as a Master in Business or a CPA certificate. By acquiring additional skills, you can make yourself more valuable to your company and could be the only one who can do a certain job in your company.

Nepotism

Even if you are the most qualified, in corporate America, in the short run, the most qualified person is not always the one who gets the job, given discrimination, nepotism and other barriers. However, over time the person who can do the best job will eventually ascend to the position that maximizes their abilities. This will occur because in a competitive labor market, if you do not maximize your employee's talents, someone else will and you will be at a competitive disadvantage.

Seeking a Job

Probably the best job you can do is the one you are most interested in and trained in. Know your interest. Know what makes you tick. Everyone has an interest, a dream, and a goal. Sometimes they are hard to find and recognize and sometimes you know what they are. One way to find out or confirm what you like is to try different events, activities, venues and jobs. Investigate anything that you think you may remotely have an interest in. Do it often and early in your life, but keep in mind no matter how old you are, it is never too late to try something new.

A Natural Talent

Once you have zeroed in on an activity you like, try and relate it to a career. Some careers are god given and natural and some have to be developed. For example, for years, I tried to run the 100-yard dash in under 10 seconds. No matter how I trained, I could never run that fast. Based on my speed, I was not destined to be a National Football League wide receiver. Another example is my short singing career. My high school counselor put me in the school choir even though I could not hold a note. I actually think they were trying to keep me out of a college prep class, but that is another chapter. Anyway, no matter how I rehearsed, the notes just were not there. I was not destined to be a lead singer or even a background support singer. Speed and song were not among my God given gifts. On the other hand, there are some individuals that can carry a note in a typhoon or can run like the relationship between distance and time was the same. If you have one of these natural born talents take advantage of it. Do not let your natural talent go to waste. I once heard of a girl who could sing like a bird but because she was very shy and feared failure, she refused to pursue a career in music. I do not know where that music career may have taken her but the job she was working was a dead end job that she did not like and was not suited to her abilities. It would have been better for her to try and fail than to not try at all. People are given a talent for a reason and even if it is not your main interest, it could be a way to a more interesting career. There is nothing wrong with a doctor who was once a singer or a Senator who once played basketball or even a President who was once an actor.

You are what you make yourself

For those of us who do not have obvious natural born talents, the career search might take a little longer. I spent 13 years in college in pursuit of a career. As I approach senior citizen age, I am still not sure of the career I want, but one thing has remained constant. I have always wanted to leave the planet in better shape when I go than when I came.

Your goals may not take a lifetime to achieve but you can almost bet that in order to achieve these goals, it will take commitment and sacrifice. You are what you make yourself. Also, never give up on your goals. **Time plus commitment equals success.**

Where are the Jobs?

Government and private organizations project where the future jobs will be. I have listed some of them in Figure 4.3 below. You should review the list and select the job that interest you and determine the following:
1) How can I commit myself to doing the best job?
2) How can I qualify to do the job?
3) How can I acquire the resources in order to qualify for the job?
4) How will this job advance my goals?

An additional list of jobs is included in the appendix of this book.

Keep one thing in mind. If you want a particular job or career, let no one talk you out of it. Try, try and try again to get the training or education or inside track required to get the job.

Figure 4.3 Part I

<u>**Occupations with the fastest Growth (In thousands)**</u>

Occupations	Percent change	Number of new jobs (in thousands)	Wages (May 2008 median)	Education or Training
Biomedical engineers	72	11.6	$77,400	Bachelor's degree
Network system and data communications analysts	53	155.8	71,100	Bachelor's degree
Home health aides	50	460.9	20,460	Short-term on-the-job training
Personal and home care aides	46	375.8	19,180	Short-term on-the-job training
Financial examiners	41	11.1	70,930	Bachelor's degree
Medical scientist, except epidemiologists	40	44.2	72,590	Doctoral degree
Physician assistants	39	29.2	81,230	Master's degree
Skin care specialists	38	14.7	28,730	Post secondary vocational
Biochemists and biophysicists	37	8.7	82,840	Doctoral degree
Athletic trainers	37	6.0	39,640	Bachelor's degree

Figure 4.3 Part II

<u>**Occupations with the fastest Growth (In thousands)**</u>

Occupations	Percent change	Number of new jobs (in thousands)	Wages (May 2008 median)	Education or Training
Physical therapist aides	36	16.7	23,760	Short-term on-the-job training
Dental hygienists	36	62.9	66,570	Associate degree
Veterinary technologists and technicians	36	28.5	28,900	Associate degree
Dental assistants	36	105.6	$32,380	Moderate-term on-the-job training
Computer software engineers, applications	34	175.1	85,430	Bachelor's degree
Medical assistants	34	163.9	28,300	Moderate-term on-the-job training
Physical therapist assistants	33	21.2	46,140	Associate degree
Veterinarians	33	19.7	79,050	First professional degree

Figure 4.3 Part III

Occupations with the fastest Growth (In thousands)

Occupations	Percent change	Number of new jobs (in thousands)	Wages (May 2008 median)	Education or Training
Self-enrichment education teachers	32	81.3	35,720	Work experience in a related occupation
Compliance officers, except agriculture, construction, health and safety, and transportation	31	80.8	48,890	Long –term on-the-job training

Source: BLS Occupational Employment Statistics and Division of Occupational Outlook

Figure 4.3

Occupations with the largest numerical growth (In thousands) Part I

Occupations	Percent change	Number of new jobs (in thousands)	Wages (May 2008 median)	Education or Training
Registered nurses	22	581.5	62,450	Associate degree
Home health aides	50	460.9	20460	Short-term on-the-job training
Customer service representatives	18	399.5	29,860	Moderate-term on-the-job training
Combined food preparation and serving workers, including fast food	15	394.3	16,430	Short-term on-the-job training
Personal and home care aides	46	375.8	19,180	Short-term on-the-job training
Retail salespersons	8	374.7	20,510	Short-term on-the-job training
Office clerks, general	12	358.7	25,320	Short –term on-the-job training
Accountants and auditors	22	279.4	59,430	Bachelor's degree
Nursing aides, orderlies, and attendants	19	276.0	23,850	Postsecondary vocational award
Postsecondary teachers	15	256.9	58,830	Doctoral degree

Source: BLS Occupational Employment Statistics and Division of Occupational Outlook

Figure 4.3

Occupations with the largest numerical growth (In thousands) Part II

Occupations	Percent change	Number of new jobs (in thousands)	Wages (May 2008 median)	Education or Training
Construction laborers	20	255.9	28,520	Moderate-term on-the-job training
Elementary school teachers, except special education	16	244.2	49,330	Bachelor's degree
Truck drives, heavy and tractor-trailer	13	232.9	37,270	Short-term on-the-job training
Landscaping and grounds keeping	18	217.1	23,150	Short-term on-the-job training
Bookkeeping, accounting, and auditing clerks	10	212.4	32,510	Moderate-term on-the-job training
Executive secretaries and administrative assistants	13	204.4	40,030	Work experience in a related occupation
Management analysts	24	178.3	73,570	Bachelor's or higher degree, plus work experience

Figure 4.3

<u>**Occupations with the largest numerical growth (In thousands) Part III**</u>

Occupations	Percent change	Number of new jobs (in thousands)	Wages (May 2008 median)	Education or Training
Computer software engineers, applications	34	175.1	85,430	Bachelor's degree
Receptionists and information clerks	15	172.9	24,550	Short-term on-the-job training
Carpenters	13	165.4	38,940	Long-term on-the-job training

Source: BLS Occupational Employment Statistics and Division of Occupational Outlook

Figure 4.3

Occupations with the fastest decline (In thousands) Part I

Occupations	Percent change	Number of new jobs (in thousands)	Wages (May 2008 median)	Education or Training
Textile bleaching and dyeing machine operators and tenders	-45	-7.2	$23,680	Moderate-term on-the-job training
Textile winding, twisting, and drawing out machine setters, operators, and tenders	-41	-14.2	23,970	Moderate-term on-the-job training
Textile knitting and weaving , machine setters, operators, and tenders	-39	-11.5	25,400	Long-term on-the-job training
Shoe machine operators and tenders	-35	-1.7	25,090	Moderate-term on-the-job training
Extruding and forming machine setters, operators, and tenders, synthetic and glass fibers	-34	-4.8	31,160	Moderate-term on-the-job training

Source: BLS Occupational Employment Statistics and Division of Occupational Outlook

Figure 4.3

Occupations with the fastest decline (In thousands) Part II

Occupations	Percent change	Number of new jobs (in thousands)	Wages (May 2008 median)	Education or Training
Sewing machine operators	-34	-71.5	19,870	Moderate-term on-the-job training
Semiconductor processors	-32	-10.0	32,230	Postsecondary vocational award
Textile cutting machine setters, operators, and tenders	-31	-6.0	$22,620	Moderate-term on-the-job training
Postal Services mail sorters, processors, processing machine operators	-30	-54.5	50,020	Short-term on-the-job training
Fabric menders, except garment	-30	-0.3	28,470	Moderate-term on-the-job training
Wellhead pumpers	-28	-5.3	37,860	Moderate-term on-the-job training
Fabric and apparel patternmakers	-27	-2.2	37,760	Long-term on-the-job training

Source: BLS Occupational Employment Statistics and Division of Occupational Outlook

Figure 4.3

Occupations with the fastest decline (In thousands) Part III

Occupations	Percent change	Number of new jobs (in thousands)	Wages (May 2008 median)	Education or Training
Drilling and boring machine tool setters, operators, tenders, metal and plastic	-27	-8.9	30,850	Moderate-term on-the-job training
Lathe, turning machine tool setters, operators, tenders, metal	-27	-14.9	32,940	Moderate-term on-the-job training
Order clerks	-26	-64.2	27,990	Short-term on-the-job training
Coil winders, tapers, and finishers	-25	-5.6	27,730	Short-term on-the-job training
Photographic processing machine operators	-24	-12.5	$20,360	Short-term on-the-job training
File clerks	-23	-49.6	23,800	Short-term on-the-job training
Derrick operators, oil and gas	-23	-5.8	41,920	Moderate-term on-the-job training

Source: BLS Occupational Employment Statistics and Division of Occupational Outlook

Where the jobs are not

Several industries listed below in Figure 4.4 should not be considered as good career moves. At best, they should be used as stepping-stones to better paying jobs. They should be jobs you take to pay for a college education or to fill the income gaps before or between jobs. These jobs are at the lower end of the pay scale and offer limited opportunities for growth.

Even as I discourage long-term employment in these areas, I also encourage you to keep an eye open on the opportunities within these jobs or any job market. Someone once said that one man's junk is another man's treasure. In every situation, there is opportunity for growth. Take for instance agriculture. Although this industry is losing workers, people still have to eat so they will still need farm produce. The task is to migrate from the small mom and pop farms to the large corporate farms. Some of the large corporate farms do more than just grow food; they also transport, market and sell food. By consolidating small farms into large and cost efficient farm corporations, an unprofitable and job declining sector of the economy can be made profitable and deliver a superior food product.

Figure 4.4

Numeric change in Wages and Salary Employment in Goods-producing Industries, 2008 – 2018 (projected)

Industries	Employment
Construction	+1,337,000
Agriculture, forestry, fishing and hunting	-17,000
Mining, quarrying, and oil and gas extraction	-104,000
Manufacturing	-1,206,000

Source: BLS National Employment Matrix

Summary of Chapter 4 - Employment and Unemployment

1) The unemployment rate for Blacks is nearly twice the national average for at least the last 38 years.
2) Blacks must build their business community from the ground up.
3) You will have to be skilled and educated to get a job in the future.
4) The best job is probably one that you are most interested in and trained in.
5) Look for a job group that is projected to grow in the future.
6) Avoid job groups that are expected to decline in the future.

Chapter 5 – Income Producing Assets:

Income producing assets vs. non-income producing assets

Income producing assets are those assets that increase your net-worth. The increase can come in the form of property that earns revenue or property that appreciates in value or both. One of the income producing assets that can produce both revenue and appreciation is rental property. An added benefit with this type of property is the possibility that you can also reduce your federal, state and local taxes.

No one should rent

Renting is sometime a necessary evil but it should be limited to a short period of time, say less than a year. Even over short periods, renting can be **wealth inefficient**. For example, I once rented a 400 square feet studio apartment for fifteen months at $1,400.00 a month. Total rent was $21,000.00. I then moved from the apartment and purchased a 1,500 square feet townhouse in the same town with 5% down. Nine months later, I sold the townhouse for $37,000.00 more than I had paid for it. Also, because I lived in the townhouse, I was able to deduct nearly all of my monthly loan payment because it was mostly interest, from my taxes. By purchasing a home, my net-worth increased $37,000.00 and I was able to reduce my taxes by thousands of dollars. In contrast, when I moved out of the apartment, the $21,000.00 in rent money I had paid went from my net-worth to the landlord's net-worth. I lost $21,000.00 by renting. By owning, I gained $37,000.00 plus the tax write off, a $58,000.00 swing in my direction.

Build wealth

The $37,000.00 earned through appreciation on one piece of property is not the end of the financial event but only the beginning. That money went into the purchase of another home that has since appreciated $300,000.00. Because of this amount, banks are willing to loan money at favorable rates up to and in some cases more than the equity value in the new property.

This sum was not earned by working hard every day but rather working smart and being in a position to take advantage of opportunities. Place yourself in the right place and the right time.

Be prepared for the Long Run

Property values can also go down but keep in mind the old saying; they are not making any more land so in the long run property will go up. Also do not forget the three main principles of real-estate which are location, location, location.

Put yourself in a position to take advantage of your opportunities

With bad credit, no bank would have approved a loan for 5% at a low interest rate. Without the loan, the $300,000.00 in appreciation would not have been realized. **In America, good credit is king.** The start of any financial planning starts with your credit standing. This information can be determined often at no cost or a small charge by contacting one of the credit companies listed below.

1) EquiFax: www.equifax.com
2) Experian (TRW) 888-397-3742
3) Trans Union 800-888-4213

Always maintain good credit. It is your passport to financial independence.

Wear Your Jewelry in Your Wallet

Earrings, necklaces, charms, bracelets, rings and other body ornaments all cost money and add little worth to your portfolio. Avoid these types of expenditures. This is an expenditure that does not generate revenue and usually loses its value over time. You would be better off buying government bonds or some other asset that will generate revenue or will appreciate in value.

The only jewelry I would recommend would be a plain wedding band. I recommend a wedding band because it is a symbol that you are married and that you respect your marriage. If I had followed my own advice, the $2,000 I spent on wedding bands with diamonds would have been invested. Today, that investment could be worth a lot more than the diamond studded wedding bands.

As it is the diamonds are valued less today than when I purchased them twelve years ago.
Jewelry does not generate income. The purchase of jewelry takes income away.

Car Purchase

A few years ago, I was riding with a friend of mine and I told him that Blacks should not spend their money on fancy cars but should instead buy less expensive car and save and invest the difference. His comment to me was that Blacks have very little to show to the world that they are somebody and driving an expensive car is a way to try and do that.

I appreciate his comment but not his results. Cars depreciate as soon as they leave the showroom. You are losing money the day you make your first payment and it only gets worse from there considering the cost of maintenance, insurance and license for the car. Also, the more you pay for a car the more these extra cost can be. Some states base their license fees on the value of your car. Insurance and maintenance charges also can be based on the amount the car cost.

A car should be purchased to meet your utility not your ego.

If I had listened to this advice, I would probably be nearly rich today. I did purchase an expensive used car and it cost me. It cost me in maintenance. The only saving grace with the purchase is that the car went for twelve years and 190,000 miles. This meant that I did not have a car note for eight years. So I conclude that if you do buy an expensive car make sure that it will last a long time, so you do not always have a car note. **Get your money's worth**.

Spend Your Money Wisely

Alcohol, Illegal Drugs and Smoking abuse is costing the Black Community nearly $53,000,000,000 Billion per year.

Blacks spend nearly 53 billion dollars per year see (Figure 5.2) below on alcohol; drugs and smoking that offers little return. In fact they are negative purchases because they take away from your ability to earn money or reduce expenses. For example, alcohol will not only cost you money but will also make you inefficient on the job, which reduces your income. A person can become so dependent on drugs that they will spend every dollar they have to get it. Smoking is costly and it can increase your health cost and take your life. See information below Figure 5.1 from the National Institute on Drug Abuse (NIDA) and the Centers for Disease Control (CDC) on the annual cost of alcohol, drugs and smoking.

The NIDA, a component of the U.S. Department of Health & Human Services estimates that the cost of alcohol abuse   was 166.5 billion, see Figure 5.1. Drug abuse was estimated at 109.8 billion. The cost included lost of earning (productivity), loss of earning while being incarcerated, criminal justice & highway safety, private and public health insurance, life insurance, tax payments, pensions, social welfare insurance, and the cost of crime.

The CDC - Centers for Disease Control estimates the medical cost associated with smoking at 75 billion a year and lost productivity at 80 billion a year.

Figure 5.1

<u>Annual Cost of Alcohol & Drug Abuse and Smoking</u>

Alcohol Abuse	$ 166,500,000,000
Drug Abuse	$ 109,800,000,000
Smoking	$ 155,000,000,000
Total	$ 431,300,000,000

Source: NIDA and CDC

Figure 5.2

Alcohol Abuse, Illegal Drug Abuse, and Smoking Cost for a year (Billions)

Race	% Of US Population 2010	Total Cost	Alcohol	Illegal Drugs	Smoking
Black	12.2	52.6	20.3	13.4	18.9
White	64.7	279.0	107.7	71.0	100.3
Hispanic	16.0	69.1	26.7	17.6	24.8
Other	7.1	30.6	11.8	7.8	11.0
Total	100.0	431.3	166.5	109.8	155.0

Source: NIDA and CDC

The numbers in table one are based on the percentage of the race in the general population. In some cases, race percentage may not equal abuse but it does reflect an approximation to the actual.

Dysfunctional Purchases

Spending $53,000,000,000 on booze, drugs and tobacco products is not a good investment. This amount alone is enough to build the Black economy and put every Black person to work, end poverty, end crime and create a society where everyone has a future. The Black community should shift this money from the non-income or dysfunctional purchase that it is to an income producing purchase by investing these resources in Black businesses.

Gambling - Another Non Income Producing Purchase

With gambling you might as well take your money out of your pocket and throw it into the wind. When gambling, the odds are not with you. It does not matter if it's the casinos, racetrack or even the state lottery. The house will win most of the time which is why you will seldom see a gambling operation go broke but you will see individuals lose their pay checks or even life savings to gambling addiction. Blacks gamble away millions of dollars each year.

These dollars could be used to pay for college, housing or just the monthly utility bill. Because many Blacks are so far behind economically, any dollars wasted on gambling are amplified and the loss is even bigger to the community.

Functional Purchases

1) Buy a home or condominium vs. renting an apartment.
2) Buy assets that will generate income and over the long run will appreciate like government bonds or property vs. jewelry that will decline in value.
3) Purchase a car only when it is necessary and only one that meets basic needs. Also, look for a car with the lowest cost and the greatest utility.

Maximize Income

Money is a must have in America as well as for most of the rest of the world. If you do not have a lot of it, then what you do have, you need to make sure that you get the maximum utilization from it.

To grow financially, you need to take in more than you pay out. Listed below are some every day practices you can employ to build wealth.

1) Buy a home rather than rent. By owning a home, you can build equity and provide an asset that usually appreciates. Also, home ownership can provide comfort and financial security for your family. In addition, home ownership can reduce your federal, state, and local taxes.

2) Until you become rich, buy only the amount of car you need to meet your minimum transportation needs. Remember cars do not usually appreciate. They usually depreciate from the moment you leave the car dealer's lot. The money you save on not **over** buying could be your ticket to wealth. For example, if you buy a $30,000 dollar car when a $15,000 car meets your needs, then you could be over spending by $15,000 dollars plus interest charges. The $15,000 you did not put into a depreciating asset like a car could be used to build or buy a business, which could earn you millions of dollars. Some of the most successful companies in the nation were started with much less than $15,000. There is one thing that America

offers and that is an opportunity to become rich if you develop a product or service that the public needs or wants. Just ask the founders of Microsoft or Apple.

3) Do not sell products or services that will bring harm to your customer or their community like foods high in fat, sodium, and cholesterol. Do not sell products like alcohol that has led to spouse and child abuse and family disintegration. The Black and poor communities need companies they can trust to provide goods and services that enrich their lives and protect their families.

Summary of Chapter 5 – Income Producing Assets

1) Accumulate income-producing assets. Minimize the purchase of non-income producing assets.
2) Do not rent. Renting transfers your wealth to someone else.
3) Build wealth.
4) Credit is king. Put yourself in a position to take advantage of your opportunities. Maintain good credit.
5) Dysfunctional Purchases are a waste.
6) Don't waste your money on booze, drugs, tobacco or gambling.

Chapter 6 – Communication:

> **Blacks find themselves today without the communication companies necessary to define their own destiny.**

Communications can Galvanize Black Goals and Aspirations

Communication is the link that ties together your family, your community, your job, your business, and your stake in the world. Without it, a person, group or a race are uncoordinated, unfocused and subject to the goals and ambitions of others. Others often use their coordination to manipulate and control the uncoordinated. Today, Blacks find themselves in the uncoordinated group because they do not have the communication structure to galvanize their goals and aspirations.

Communication is the Corner Stone of Organization

Bring it all together through communication. It is absolutely necessary for Blacks to own their own communication network in order to address the needs of the Black community. In the past, Blacks have depended on others to communicate the needs of the Black community. This approach has **not** lead to the development of the communication structure needed to build large Black corporations, schools, hospitals and all of the other structures needed to maintain and grow a community.

Communications is the tool that allows a group to organize and pool its resources and direct those resources toward a common goal. The goal can be to build a business or an industry. The goal can also be to prevent an outside group from selling harmful products like alcohol, tobacco products and drugs to the community. Another communication goal can be to protect the community from harmful massages like stereotyping Blacks as lazy, stupid or frightened, as the motion picture, advertising, television industries have attempted to do.

For Over a Century, the Movie Industry has Stereotyped Blacks

The media have used their communication power to portray Blacks in a negative way. Take for example the movie industry. For over a century, they have portrayed Blacks as weak, frightened, stupid, lazy and illiterate. You only have to look at the countless movies, TV shows, news programs and commercials to confirm this problem. The media started early with shows presenting Blacks in subordinate positions such as maids, butlers and chauffeurs. The early shows included 'The Jack Benny Show' with its Black butler. This set the stereotype for Blacks on TV and in the movies. The trend continued with the movie 'Gone With the Wind' and its slap-able Black maid, and who could ever forget 'Driving Miss Daisy' with its Black chauffeur at the wheel. Blacks are seldom shown as presidents, captains, scientist and lawyers. Blacks are most often shown as buffoons and clowns, many unable to speak well and often illiterate, weak, afraid and cowardly. This stereotype has left negative impressions in the minds of everyone who has come into contact with the movie and TV industry. A Black controlled media can end this stereotyping.

Radios of Bad English and Habits

The radio industry has not been much better for Blacks than the movie industry. Often their announcers and programming promote poor English and bad habits. If a young person is listening to these shows there is not much chance that they will learn anything, but how to speak poorly and act like a fool.

I once listened to a Black announcer telling his audience how to pay your bills late and not be charged. What we need are radio stations that will encourage their audience not to create unnecessary bills and never make a bill you cannot pay on time.

Blacks must build a Positive and Effective Media

ABC, CBS, NBC, FOX, CNN, CNBC and MSNBC seldom present Blacks in a favorable story. Usually the only time that you will see a Black person on their news channels is when they are in orange prison jump suit, in handcuffs and are under arrest.

Due to the negative images produced by the current media, it is necessary for the Black community to build a communication system that will present Blacks and other people of color in a positive manner.

Currently, there are few major or national media outlets controlled by African Americans that presents Blacks in a positive way and provides the type of information the Black community needs to grow and flourish. As Blacks build these communication centers, it is paramount that they provide relevant and accurate information.

Information Relevant to the Black Community is a Must

Just as important as establishing a media that promotes Blacks is one that presents information that is relevant to the Black community. Take for example network reporting on the economy. Currently, they will report the unemployment rate of the nation at 9% but in the Black community, the actual unemployment rate is nearly twice the national average. If you were not aware of this difference and you are Black, the recession that you feel is not the conditions that are reported on the news. Blacks need a news station that reports the conditions in the Black community.

Accurate and Complete News Builds Trust

A free and unbiased media is essential to a people struggling to escape poverty. The Black community needs information that it can rely on. It needs to know what is behind the news. If there is an environmental disaster, what or who caused it? If politicians want to go to war, what lead up to this situation and what are the alternatives? If the lights go off, who is to blame? Also needed is more information on how the world views a particular situation. We live in a world community and need to know global viewpoints and perspectives.

Blacks Need Proactive News

The Black community also needs a news media that not only reports the news, but also presents recommendations on how to improve a negative news story and enhance a positive news story. For instance, if a Black man is accused of a crime, the news station should not only report the crime but also present reasons on why they think the crime occurred and what steps the community can take to prevent the crime from happening again. Steps like improving the education and job opportunities in the community or reducing the use of drugs or alcohol. The evening news does not have to be all about what when wrong. It can also report how to make things go right. This would encourage the Black community to do more of what is right than what is wrong.

Black Media Can Help Break the Cycle of Crime

Currently, the legal system is structured to catch a person who commits a crime and lock the person up. Once in prison, if a person does not receive the proper rehabilitation, they could still represent a danger to society once released. Also, because they are in prison, they have the chance to pick up some additional bad habits and could be worse off when released than when they when into prison. This could lead to even more serious crimes and arrest. Society would then end up just were it started.

The black community cannot afford this recycling and needs to break the cycle. That is why it is important that society learns from each person who commits a crime and takes a positive step to prevent the crime from recurring. Today's media does not ask the question why the crime was committed. Also, it does not present suggestions on how to prevent the crime from happening again. The only suggestions they might have are to hire more police or start a neighbor watch program. These two solutions do not address the reasons why a crime was committed in the first place. It would be the job of a pro-active Black news media to go behind the story and determine why the crime happened and make recommendations on how to prevent the crime from happening again.

Black Owned Communication Companies

Listed below (Figure 6.1) are some of the largest owned Black communication companies. In order to provide the scope and type of news the Black community needs, these companies will have to grow and more Black companies will have to be developed. Competition from White companies is enormous but surmountable. Three of the largest White companies are listed below in (Figure 6.2). One of these companies, Viacom is so large that it even bought out one of the largest Black companies BET.

Also of the five largest Black communication companies listed in Figure 6.1 two are no longer Black owned. Essence Communications Partner was purchased by Time Inc. and Granite Broadcasting Corporation declared bankruptcy in 2006 and was purchased by Silver Point Capital.

Additionally Johnson Publishing Co. Inc. has lost customers and is trying to survive. One positive note, Oprah Winfrey has started Oprah Winfrey Network (OWN).

It is crucial that Blacks build communication companies. Without a voice, the needs of the Black community will not be heard.

Figure 6.1

Largest Black Communication Companies

Company	Type of Business	Location	Year Started	Staff	Sales (In Millions)
Johnson Publishing Co. Inc.	Publishing, TV production, cosmetics & hair care	Chicago, IL	1942	1,676	$488,455
Radio One Inc.	Owns & operates radio stations	Lanham, MD	1980	1800	344,650
Rush Communications of NYC Inc.	Entertainment, fashion, advertising & publishing	New York, NY	1991	180	320,000
Essence Communications Partners	Magazine publishing and entertainment	New York, NY	1969	143	136,150
Granite Broadcasting Corp.	Broadcasting, sale of commercial air time to advertisers	New York, NY	1988	714	130,046

Source: Black Enterprise Magazine June 2004 issue.

The Appliance Business isn't what it used to be.

White corporate America started small and grew by expanding their product line and going into new products that compliment their existing products, see Figure 6.2. They also used money generated from their core business to buy and build into other businesses. Take for example General Electric. GE started selling dishwashers and they now sell jet engines. The cash and property from these businesses bought them the power to gain national broadcasting rights and the ability to acquire NBC, (now partly owned by Comcast), CNBC, MSNBC and other communication companies. They can now sell their products on their own stations. They can also control the media on how their products are presented. They have total control, from the raw materials needed to build their products to the media coverage needed to sell their products.

Figure 6.2

<u>**White Communication Companies**</u>

Company	Type of Business	Location	Year Started	Staff	Sales (In Billions)
General Electric	Energy, Aircraft engines, Appliances, Finance, Medical Systems	Fairfield, CT	1892	304,000	157,000,000
Disney	ABC, ESPN, Miramax Files, Disneyland, Disney World	Burbank, CA	1923	149,000	38,063,000
Viacom	CBS, BET, Paramount Pictures, UPN, MTV, Rhapsody	New York, NY	1986	11,900	13,000,000

Black Companies Do not Grow, White Companies Do

When you compare Black companies with White companies the disparity in growth between the companies is obvious. For example, Johnson Publishing the Black company started in 1942 has 1,676 employees and generates $488,455,000 million in revenue. Viacom, the White company started in 1986 has 11,900 employees and generates $13,000,000,000 billion in revenue. Comparing other Black companies with White companies, you get similar results. With size comes power. Viacom and Disney growth provided them with strong financial and political power. They used this power to buy major television stations, CBS and ABC respectively. They are now in a position to expand and sell to every household in the country and in the world. By using their size they can sell more of their goods and services, which allow them to become even bigger.

In order for Blacks to determine their own destiny, they will have to control the communications in their community. In order to do that, Black communication companies will have to grow and become dominate in their community.

The Disney Model

Disney employs 149,000 people and the company generated $38,063,000,000 billion dollars in 2009. Their communication staff alone is larger than all of the Black communication companies combined.
There is no reason why Black companies cannot use the same model that Disney used to grow with some modifications. The benefits to the Black communities would be race changing. Blacks would be transformed from the back of the bus to owning the bus and the bus line. Millions of jobs would be created and the grip of poverty would be broken on the Black race.

The Internet

Everyone should become an Internet user. It is one of the greatest communication inventions of our time. It does not matter whether you live on the banks of the Mississippi, the slums of New York, the gold coast of Chicago or the suburbs of Los Angeles. Anyone at anytime can be in constant communications with anyone else in the country. You can stay in touch with your family and friends or find a business or career on the Internet. You can run a business from the Internet by setting up web sites to sell your products or services. The Internet has information about finances, health, government, shopping, news and just about any other subject you can think of. What I like most about the Internet is that it is not controlled by three or four network news channels, which are all White-owned. Now Blacks can create their own news outlets on the Internet at very little cost and still achieve a wide circulation. The only thing Black viewers have to do is use the Internet as their source and distribution of information, and instantly, a Black communication industry is born.

Summary of Chapter 6 - Communications

1) Size is paramount. The larger the size of an organization the more people that company can hire and the more resources it can command.

2) News programming must be unbiased if they are to be effective. Communications in the Black community must be free of any outside forces and free to report the news accurately and completely. The growth of the Black community depends on receiving good information so that it can make good decisions.

3) Blacks need to build communication companies that will present them in positive roles and leadership positions. The current media that shows Blacks in negative roles in the motives, on television, in advertising must be replaced.

4) Blacks need relevant information from its news channels. Information that they can use to support their families and build their companies and communities.

5) Needed are pro-active news stations that not only present the news but makes recommendations on how to improve problems in the community.

6) The Internet is a cheap and fast way to build a communication company.

Chapter 7 – Education:

The public school system in the Black community represents one of the greatest failures of our time.

Education is the Gateway to Prosperity

One of the best investments a parent can make for their child is to ensure that they get a good education. Without an education in today's world, you can expect a life of poverty since jobs requiring little education have gone the way of the steel mills and textile factory, out of the country. Because many Black children do not speak well, they have less of a chance to learn how to read and write and thus get a good education.

Black children score the lowest on the national test in reading and writing. I think that a lot of this is because they are constantly exposed to poor English. Even if they are taught good English in the classroom, the movie industry, television advertisements, their peers and even there family exposes them to bad English.

It is important that Black children are immersed in good English. Good English skills will lead to good writing, reading and speaking skills. With these skills, they will perform better in school, which will decrease their drop out rate and increase their graduation rate.

An educated Black child is a benefit, not only to the child but also to the community. Uneducated Black children cost the child and the nation. Uneducated Black children make up a large percentage of the poor and criminal population. Currently over 11 percent of young Black men have been in prison, most of them poor and uneducated. In some states, over 50% of the prison populations are Black men. Black unemployment is nearly twice the nation average. Black poverty is almost three times the national average. This condition is costing the nation billions of dollars in police, court systems and prisons. Billions more are spend on car, house and business insurance to cover the crimes committed by the mostly poor and uneducated. These billions of dollars do not even measure the untold suffering resulting from broken lives, deaths and injuries to victims and criminals. I believe that the cure to this malaise starts with the school system. An educated person today is a contributor to society tomorrow. On the other hand, an uneducated person today is a cost to society tomorrow.

Education Starts at Home

The parent is primarily responsible for the education of the child between birth and the age of five. Usually after five the child enters school and the school along with the parent is responsible for educating children. Around ten years of age, the child, parent and the school is responsible for producing an educated adult. Let's look at each of these stages and construct the building blocks needed to successfully complete each stage.

Birth to Five - Parent Responsibility

During this phase, most of the environment that a child is exposed to comes from their parent. Because of this it is important that the environment is positive, educational and safe.

Do you wonder why you handle situations a certain way? Why you automatically take out the trash if you are a male or you automatically shop for food if you are a female. Or you do not hit your child for doing something you feel is wrong or you do punish your child in this manner. Chances are, you have observed these characteristics in your parent. At a young age, the child is learning and will pick up the mannerism of the parents. What you do is what your child is likely to do. This is why a parent should not fight in front of their kids or behind their kids for that matter. The home should be a place where differences are resolved through negotiations and compromise. The positive should be emphasized, even when things are not going as planned. Remember, your child is always watching and learning and your child will probably be a produce of your actions.

Ebonics, Black English, Ghetto talk, Destroys Education

Learning starts at home. If the parent is speaking poor English, it is very likely that the child will also speak poor English and a poor ability to speech in America is a prescription to poverty. Ebonics, Black English, grotto English, swearing all robs your child of the ability to communicate to the outside world. If a child has been exposed to these forms of bad English, when the child enters elementary school, they will already be below the national reading level and could need a life time to catch up which in many cases they do not. In the Black community poor grammar can be found everywhere. Since children are with their parents most of the time, if the parent is speaking poor English, there is a good chance that the child will speak poor English. When this occurs, the parent can be one of the worst influences on their kids. Other areas where Black children are exposed to poor English is in the church, on the playground, on the public bus, in the supermarket, in pre school, in day care, from the baby sitter, from the television and any other venue where illiteracy is tolerated and encouraged. In order to educate your child, <u>avoid areas where poor English is used.</u>

Improve your Learning Environment

Listed below are some everyday things you can do to improve your learning environment.

1) If parents do not speak well themselves, you can listen to people who can speak well. It is not that important what they are saying but how they say it. Newscasters normally speak well. They have to sound creditable. College instructors and public speakers usually have a command of English. There are public speaking clubs that promote good speaking.

2) The church is one of the most prominent institutions of the Black community. It is also one of the most influential in the Black community. If the pastor is not speaking good English, than that sends a message to the hold congregation, that good English is not importance. If this happens than, Sunday after Sunday, sermon after sermon, believer after believer is

indoctrinated in poor English. The poor speaking habits are than taken home and repeated over and over in an endless recycling of illiteracy. Pastors need to speak good English so that their congregation hears and repeats good English. If your pastor is not speaking good English, than work with him or her to make them aware of the need for your family and the community to live in an environment that promotes good communication. If your pastor or church does not change, than you do not have to choose between god and prosperity, you can simply find another church that is literate and you can have god and prosperity.

3) When selecting a baby sitter, interview the person and ensure that they speak good English. After all, your child will also learn from the sitter, the good and the bad.

4) Television. This is the one place that combines racism with illiteracy. Even the cartoons on television show Black children as illiteracy. TV can un-teach in one afternoon all the good English you have exposed your child to in a month. A parent should avoid any program that does not present a child as being literate. Literate means the persons or things in the show are speaking good English.

5) Pre-school, day care centers all must be monitor for good English. They should be areas of learning but do not take that for granted. Find out their teaching methods. Determine if they know what learning is or are they just warehousing your child. You may have to start you own school and staff it with mothers and fathers interested in providing a good learning environment.

The Public School System

The public school system in the Black community represents one of the greatest failures of our time. The school system is committed more to paying the salaries of its teachers than to the education of its students. It is better at finding excuses for failure than at solving problems for success. Year after year, they say they are going to be better, but year after year and student after student they get worse. There are many charts and graphs to confirm the denigrating public school system but you only have to listen to the student's speech and look how they dress and act to see if they are being prepared for college or a life of crime. A high school student being prepared for college will speak and look professional, like a doctor, engineer, lawyer, or scientist. A student who speaks poor English and looks more like a drug dealer is being prepared for a life of crime.

The Teachers and Administrators are to Blame

Why is it that these school administrators can be paid a salary and not produce a good product? There are many excuses why Black students score the lowest on nation reading, writing, math and science test. Some say it's the money per student spend by the school system. Others say it's the inadequate facilities the students are provided. Still others say the parents are not committed to their children's education. The teachers blame the parents, the parents blame the teachers and around and around we go. **I blame the deterioration of the public schools in the Black community on the teachers and their administration because they are the ones being paid to teach.** The parents are paying the school system to teach their kids and as long as the teachers are accepting a paycheck, they are responsible to produce a well-educated student. Hire good teachers and administrators and you will get good students.

Black Students are not being prepared for Tomorrows Jobs

When I was entering high school in 1957, I went to the high school consular. I wanted to know what courses I needed to go to college. I was told that my junior high school grades were not good enough for college and I would be better off getting a job in the local steel mills. I was then assigned to non-college classes; i.e. wood shop, metal shop, and all the other non-academic classes. My high school consular was preparing me for a career that I had no interest in and as it turned out no skills in and no future in. Not to many years later, the mills closed.

I believe that this is what is happening in the public school today. Black students are not being prepared for the modern jobs. Black children are being prepared for the steel mill jobs that no long exist. Black students are not being taught to speak well, dress well or relate well to a modern world that requires math, science and English. The public schools are not teaching Black students the skills they will need to compete in the modern work force. It is up to the Black parents to take over these dysfunctional school systems and transform them into institutions where Black students will learn math, science and English.

Non-funding School Improvements

There is obviously a need for funding in the school system, but there are also many non-funding activities a school system can engage in that will contribute to an educated student.

Listed below are some non-funding steps the public schools can take to improve their students:

1) Assume that all students can achieve a high level of education and prepare the school curriculum and programs to reach that level.

2) Require that all students speak good English. By telling the student that they must speak good English, you are saying that they are expected to become doctors, lawyers, executives, financial analyses, engineers, scientists, nurses, presidents and leaders. Require each student to speak in front of the class each day, so that they will become use to speaking well and it will become the normal and nature way to speak even when they are no longer in the classroom.

3) Dress code. If you dress like a thief you will probably act like a thief. If you dress like a president, you will probably act like a president. From what I can see of how the Black student dress, they will more then likely end up in the big house whether than the White house. Pants that hang off you and hair that looks like a fright show are not the beginning of well-groomed professionals. Sometimes you need to act the part to get the part. Dressing like a professional is the first step to becoming a doctor or lawyer.

4) Health. The head of any health department of any school system with any student 25 pounds overweight should be fired. Excise is cheap and there are endless venues to accomplish an excise program. From open fields, city parks, city streets, classrooms, no student has to be without excise. It is up to the schools to teach the virtue of staying in shape by eating health food and excising. School cafeterias, and vending machines should be

cleaned of food high in calories, fat, cholesterol, sodium and other un-health ingredients. Students should be taught how to stay health and why it is important to look and fell health.

School Funding

The entire community benefits from a good school system. Good school systems produce educated students who can command good jobs. These jobs generate income and property tax revenue. The tax revenue is then used to pay for services, like roads and fire protection, a service that the whole community uses. Since everyone benefits from a good school system, everyone should pay for the schools. This would include not only the parents with children in school but also the adults in the community who do not have children in the school system. Often the connection between good schools and good communities is not made. Take for example my hometown. The city officials often tried to pass a bond issue to support the schools. Almost as often, the bond issue would fail and the school system would decline. One day the good citizens look around their town to find high crime, residents feeing to the suburbs and the cost of their car and home insurance cost going through the roof. They failed to make the connection that good schools make good students and good students turn into productive workers who pay the taxes that build and maintain good communities. If they had made a small investment in their schools by pasting some of the school bond issues, they may have prevented the raising crime rate and insurance cost. Insurance cost that is now needed to protect them from the students they failed to education. Schools are no different from any other part of our society. Cost to operate increases and resources must be found and committed to cover these cost. There needs to be an agreement between the taxpayer and the school system. The school system should expect the taxpayer to cover operating expense and the taxpayer should expect the school system to deliver a well-educated student.

School Security is a Waste of Money

There are some things I think are a waste of school funds, since they do not add to the learning experience. Listed below are just a few.

1) School security. Spending school funds on security is a waste of money. The more money you spend on security the less money you have to spend on computers. Security expenditures do nothing to add to the education of a student and this type of expenditure should be avoided or minimized. If you are running a school properly, security problems will not occur.

2) Exist test are a waste of time and money. If the student has passed each grade each year, that is test enough. Why retest the student at the end of their high school on subjects their teachers have already certified that they are proficient in. If there is a problem it is not the student, it is the teacher.

3) High salaries for teachers and administrator that do not produce good students are a waste of money. Good work desires good salaries, poor work desires dismissal.

Once our student has leaned to speak good English, ware clothes that presents a professional look, has groomed hair, has studied hard in math, science, and language classes, and has an attitude that I can success no matter what the odds, it is time to select a college.

Forget the Obstacles, Go to College

I was as prepared for college as a freshman is for postgraduate work. I had no money for college and no college prep courses and a high school grade point average of "c", I figured that after one examine at college, I would be running for the door. Also, I had no encouragement to go to college. Any mention of going to college was met with there is no way you can get to college or finish college. This viewpoint came from everywhere. My high school consular said that I should not go to college. In my high school bookkeeping class, I asked the teacher if there were any bookkeeping jobs. Even though there were thousands of jobs in this area, I was advised that there were none. I believe that I was discouraged from going to college because I was Black and I believe that even today, Blacks are still discouraged from going to college.

Blacks need to be encouraged to go to college regardless of grade point average, income or family background. I believe that a higher education is a must for any student who expects to reach their full potential.

It is the job of the high school teachers and career planners to make their students aware of the benefits of a college degree. No Black student or for that matter no student should be told that they should not go to college. Don't let anyone stop you from going to college.

Where are the Best Colleges?

The best college maybe the one that let's you in.
You should try to get into the best college you can, given your finances, brains and drive. The importance thing is that you get into college. It does not matter whether the college is Ivy League or a small town school. What is important is that you get exposed to higher learning and at the same time learn what your possibilities are. When I entered college, I had no idea what my possibilities were. By the time I graduated from college, I believed that anything was possible.

The high school consular, teachers and parents should be there to help a student find the right college, but a student does not have to wait for help. A student can go to a search engine on the Internet, (I have find "Google" to be helpful) and search for colleges and universities that they would like to attend. The schools will list their requirements, cost and aid programs. It is important not to be discouraged by the school requirements. With my low grades, the only way I got into college was as a conditional student. Once I pasted my first classes the conditions were lifted and I was on my way. Keep in mind that if you want it bad enough it can be achieved.

Matching up Job with Education, Skill and Interest.

When I first when to college, I did not know what to major in. My high school consular who had discouraged me from even going to college was not about to provide a list of what I could major in. Also, coming from a family that never had a person graduate from college and only one member who even when to college, I did not have I lot of family background to draw from. In addition, not only was the family education level low in some case third grade but no one had even worked in a job other than blue collar or general labor. There was not one white-collar member of the family. In those days, companies did not hire Blacks for white-collar jobs.

I had no idea how to match up interest, skill, and education with a job. Today a good high school consular is crucial to a student's future. The consular should provide the direction, materials and encouragement to a student so that the student with their parents can may an informed decision on their future studies and career.

In order to help you identify the job market and the education you will need to qualify for the job, see again the list of jobs provided in Chapter 4 Employment and Unemployment and in the appendix.

Summary of Chapter 7 - Education

Build schools and you will not have to build prisons. The best way to reduce the prison population is to increase the school population.

1) Use good English. It will lead to good reading and writing which will lead to good grades which will lead to good jobs which will lead to good families, neighborhoods and good schools which will lead to good English.

2) Education starts at home. A child will learn from their parents first. If the parent speaks poorly the child will also speak poorly. Create a home, church and community environment that encourages good speaking, reading and writing habits.

3) Hold teachers, principles and schools superintends responsible for teaching children. Accept no excuses for failure.

4) Good teacher need good salaries. Support funding for public schools at the local, state and federal levels.

5) Go to college and finish. You can make no better investment in yourself.

72

Chapter 8 – Health & Food

"EAT FOR LIFE NOT FOR DEATH"

African Americans have one of the highest mortality rates in the country. One reason is poor eating habits.

Good health is like good business in America. A person is going nowhere without money, neither are they going anywhere without good health.

What does it take to change the poor eating habits of Blacks?

I have spent countless hours talking to just the members of my family on the need to eat healthy. My crusade against unhealthy eating started when my father had a stroke.

My father insisted on an unhealthy lifestyle of fried chicken, salty ham, alcohol and cigars. Because of this, in his seventies, he had a stroke. The stroke took away a lot of his mobility and some of his ability to speak. The medical cost to treat the stroke took most of his life savings. If he had followed a healthier life style chances are he would not have had a stroke. Also the money used to treat the stroke could have been used to advance the family such as funding his grand children's college education, or paying off his car note or making repairs to a leaky roof on his home. The money he spent on health care and not on roof repair is a good example of a missed opportunity to accumulate wealth. Because his limited resources were needed to pay for health cost, there wasn't any money left to pay for roof repair. The roof continued to leak which eventually caused the inside walls to collapse. Of course, when the walls collapsed the value of his home was reduced which reduced his estate's worth, which reduced the amount of inheritance he could pass on to his wife and children.

This is a round about way to say that his money could have been used to educate the family and build assets verses having to use his money to treat a preventable illness. What I am advocating is that you do not contribute to an early illness or an early death by consuming into your body food, booze or smoke that is harmful to you.

Moving from harmful consumption that reduces your wealth to healthy consumption that increases your wealth is like making a double jump to prosperity.

Breaking the Cycle of Poverty

The cycle of poverty in the Black and poor communities can be broken when we eat for life and not for death.

In the past, people did not know what was in the food supply. Today much of that has changed since the law requires that food ingredient be listed on food packages and containers. If you want to know what is in the food supply, you only have to read the content label. This seems like any easy way to identify foods high in fat, sodium, and cholesterol and avoid them. Getting people to read the labels seems to be the big problem. Most of the Black people, especially Black men that I have talked to about food content labels, refused to read the content information. It seems that Blacks would rather continue to eat unhealthy food now and die, than to change their diets and live.

Why do Blacks continue to eat unhealthy food? As an endless stream of Black men march to their death because of bad diets one can only wonder, what has brought them to this stage in their lives? Why do they disregard their responsibility to themselves, their wives, children, and grand children? Many Black men seem only concerned about their own pleasure and vices. Why else would they disregard the health warnings about fried chicken, barbequed beef ribs, alcohol and tobacco? I see it in my neighborhood, in my family, among my friends, Black man after Black man falling victim to poor diets and no one asking the question why.

Why haven't the Black doctor's association warned Blacks against the unhealthy diets and provide directions to a healthier lifestyle? Perhaps they are themselves dining on the ribs. Also, what about the pastors presiding over the funeral of a just departed 55-year-young Black man who died from high blood pressure? Are they warning the mourners that they could also die young if they follow an unhealthy diet? Where are civil rights groups? Where are the announcements from the NAACP or Operation Push to establish health seminars? I have heard little from the Black community leaders on how Blacks can improve their health and live longer and better. It is as if the Black community has accepted a short life span and when they are killed off at a relatively young age by preventable diseases, like high blood pressure, strokes and heart attacks, no one cares.

The life expectancy of Blacks can greatly increase simply by changing their life style and not eating fried foods, or foods high in cholesterol and salt. A longer life expectancy gives the family provider more time to care for their loved ones. Also, living a healthier life reduces medical cost, freeing up more funds for housing, education and investments.

"National read a can Day"

You are what you eat and it is evident that Black people are not eating the right food. Because the government has provided valuable information on what is in the food supply by requiring food producers to identify what is in the food they sell, see (Figure 8.1), we can know what we are eating. Consumers can take advantage of this requirement by simply reading the can or package. We need a **National read a can Day**. A day when everyone reads the health labels on the food we eat and determines what foods they should consume and how much. By knowing what is in your food, you can plan healthier meals. Listed in (Figure 8.1) below is an example of the government health label on packaged foods. Please note for all of you macaroni and cheese lovers; just one cup of this food has 250 calories, 18% of your daily-recommended fat, 10% of your cholesterol and 20% of your sodium. Two cups of macaroni and cheese at one meal will restrict what you can eat and still stay within your recommended daily portions of sodium, fat, cholesterol and calories. See (Figure 8.1) below for recommended portions.

Figure 8.1

Government Food Label for Macaroni & Cheese

Macaroni & Cheese

Nutrition Facts
Serving Size 1 cup (228g)
Serving per container 2

Amount per Serving
Calories 250   Calories from Fat 110

	% Daily Value *
Total fat 12g	18%
Saturated Fat 3g	15%
Cholesterol 30 mg	10%
Sodium 470 mg	20%
Total Carbohydrate 31g	10%
Dietary Fiber 0g	0 %
Sugar 5g	
Protein 5g	
Vitamin A	4%
Vitamin C	2%
Calcium	20%
Iron	4%

* Daily Values are based on 2,000 calories diet. Your Daily Values may be higher or lower depending on your calorie needs.

Recommend per day:

	Calories	2,000	2,500
Total Fat	Less than	65g	80g
Sat Fat	Less than	20g	25g
Cholesterol	Less than	300mg	300mg
Sodium	Less than	1,500 mg	1,500mg
Total Carbohydrates		300g	375g
Dietary Fiber		25g	30g

Note: The recommended sodium amount of 1,500 mg per day is for African American, persons 51 and older and persons with hypertension, diabetes or kidney disease. The recommendation for others is 2,300 mg per day.

Source: Dietary Guidelines for Americans, 2010
The fats, cholesterol and sodium should be limited. You should get enough of the vitamins, calcium and irons.

Recommended Calories per Day:
1) Children ages 2-6 years, women, some older adults about 1600 calories per day.
2) Older children, teen girls, active women, most men about 2,200 calories per day.
3) Teen boys, active men about 2,800 calories per day.

Source: Dietary Guidelines Advisory Committee, 2000 Report.

Calories Per Day Calculator

There are calories per day calculators that will tell you how many calories you need to maintain your current weight.
Look under recommended calories per day on the internet.

What are the Health killers?

They are foods that contribute to heart attacks, strokes, obesity and high blood pressure just to name a few of the major diseases that besiege the Black community. Excess sodium leads to high blood pressure and strokes. Cholesterol can clog arteries and cause heart attacks. Fat and excess calories contribute to obesity.

Other contributors to Bad Health:
1) Saturated fats can raise your levels of bad cholesterol, or LDL, as well as your risk of developing serious conditions like heart disease.

2) Trans fats can raise your risk of a heart attack by increasing your levels of bad cholesterol and decreasing your HDL, or "good" cholesterol. They can be worse than saturated fats.

About 90% of people with severe heart disease have one or more of four classic risk factors: smoking, diabetes, high cholesterol and high blood pressure. The majority of the 650,000 new heart attacks each year could be prevented or delayed for decades by quitting smoking, reducing cholesterol and controlling hypertension and diabetes, per researcher Eric Topol of the Cleveland Clinic Foundation.

Keep in mind the recommended amount of calories, fat, cholesterol and sodium per day, see Figure 8.2.

Figure 8.2

National Recommended calories, fat, cholesterol, sodium and fiber per day

Recommend per day:

	Calories	2,000	2,500
Total Fat	Less than	65g	80g
Sat Fat	Less than	20g	25g
Cholesterol	Less than	300mg	300mg
Sodium	Less than	2,300 mg	2,300mg
Total Carbohydrates		300g	375g
Dietary Fiber		25g	30g

Listed below by type of meal (breakfast, lunch, dinner, snacks, dessert, and beverage) is a short list of some of the foods that contribute the most toward heart attacks, strokes, obesity and high blood pressure. A complete list of food ingredients is provided by the USDA-Nutrient Data Laboratory-Agricultural Research Service web site http://www.nal.usda.gov/fnic/foodcomp/.

Breakfast Food

Breakfast, the meal that should be the start of your day can be more like the end of your life. Eggs, the one time staple of breakfast can now be the staple that seals your coffin.

A few months ago, I was having breakfast with relatives. My cousin was having what seemed to be a whole platter of eggs with an equally amount of bacon. Because I was aware of the high amount of cholesterol in eggs, I mentioned this to him. He gave me a typical Black man response, "I love my eggs and bacon and no one can stop me from eating them". Shortly, thereafter, a heart attack did stop him.

You are what you eat and many breakfast foods are hazardous to your health. Listed below in Figure 8.3 are just some of the foods that can take your breath away. Particularly, harmful are the fast food items like biscuit with eggs and sausage having 1141 mgs of sodium, 38 grams of fat, 302 mgs of cholesterol and contain 581 calories. This type of food should come with a federal warning label that states that this product can cause strokes, obesity and heart failure.

Figure 8.3 Part I:

Food Content – Breakfast

NSDA #	Food Type	Portion	Mgs Sodium	Grams Fat	Mgs Cholesterol.	Calories
21005	Biscuit with eggs & sausage	1 biscuit	1141	38.70	302	581
21025	Fast food pancakes with butter & syrup	2 pancakes	1108	13.99	58	520
21021	Fast Food English muffin, egg, cheese, Canadian bacon	1 muffin	729	12.59	234	289
11370	Potatoes, hashed brown, home prepared	1 cup	534	19.53	0	413
18003	Bagel, egg	4" bagel	449	1.87	21	247
18239	Croissant	1	424	11.97	38	231

Source: USDA

Figure 8.3 Continue Part II:

Food Content – Breakfast

NSDA #	Food Type	Portion	Mgs Sodium	Grams Fat	Mgs Cholesterol.	Calories
18367	Waffle	1	383	10.58	52	218
18274	Muffin, blueberry	1	255	3.71	17	158
18268	French toast frozen	1 slice	292	3.60	48	126
01132	Egg	1	171	7.45	215	101
10124	Bacon	3 slices	439	7.94	21	103
01001	Butter salted	1 tbsp	82	11.52	31	102
01145	Butter without salt	1 tbsp	2	11.52	31	102
04132	Margarine with salt	1 tbsp	133	11.35	0	101
08060	Cereal, Kellogg, Raisin, Bran	1 cup	362	1.53	0	195
08065	Cereal, Kellogg, Rice Kripies	1.25 cup	319	.43	0	119

Source: USDA

Lunch Food

For those who are still alive after eating the unhealthy breakfast foods, don't expect any relief from lunch food see Figure 8.4. Foods like soup, cold cuts, hamburgers, burritos and baked beans with pork are land mines full of sodium, fat and cholesterol. The bad food choices are many and it does not matter who you are or what your life style is. If you are a connoisseur of soup, prepare to choke down 1000 mgs of sodium per cup. If you like a quick cheese burger don't expect to live a long life. This product comes with a whopping 1180 mgs of sodium, 32 grams of obesity graded fat, 88mgs of heart stopping cholesterol and 563 diet-busting calories. For the father taking his son out for an afternoon ballgame, the purchase of two hotdogs comes with 670 mgs of sodium each. This is a sure way to start his son on a life of high blood pressure. Also, let's not forget those wives who selected the Braunschweiger liver pork sausage for their husbands' tailgate party and cookout. If she wanted a divorce, why didn't she just ask for one instead of poisoning him with 658 mgs of sodium and 102 mgs of cholesterol per sausage?

Figure 8.4

Food Content – Lunch- Part I

NSDA #	Food Type	Portion	Sodium Mgs	Fat Grams	Cholesterol Mgs	Calories
06094	Soup-onion		3493	2.33	2	115
06067	Soup, vegetable, canned	1 cup	1010	3.70	0	122
06230	Soup, clam chowder, canned	1 cup	992	6.60	22	164
06409	Soup, beef noodle, canned	1 cup	952	3.07	5	83
06404	Soup, bean with pork	1 cup	951	5.95	3	172
06440	Soup, minestrone	1 cup	911	2.51	2	82
06243	Soup, cream of mushroom	1 cup	918	13.59	20	203
21124	Fast food submarine sandwich-cold cuts	1	1651	18.63	36	456
22904	Fast Food Chili con carne with beans	1 cup	1032	8.15	24	255
02047	Table salt		2325	0	0	0
21120	Fast food Corndog	1	973	18.90	79	460
21129	Fast food Hush puppies	5 pieces	965	11.59	135	257
21102	Fast food Chicken filled sandwich	1	957	29.45	60	515

Source: USDA

Figure 8.4

Food Content - Lunch - Part II

NSDA #	Food Type	Portion	Sodium Mgs	Fat Grams	Cholesterol Mgs	Calories
01016	Cheese cottage low fat 1%	1 cup	918	2.31	9	163
21082	Fast food Taco	1 small	1233	31.61	87	568
16123	Soy sauce	1 tbsp	914	.01	0	8
16034	Beans, Kidney, red canned	1 cup	873	.87	0	218
16011	Beans, baked with pork		1113	2.61	18	248
21098	Fast food cheeseburger	1	1108	32.94	88	563
21086	Fast food Tostada with beefs, beans, cheese	1	871	16.94	74	333
22906	Chicken pot pie frozen	1 small pie	857	29.10	41	484
15128	Fish, tuna salad	1 cup	824	18.98	27	383
21113	Hamburger	1	824	27.36	87	512
16103	Refried beans canned	1 cup	753	3.18	20	237
21118	Fast food Hotdog	1	670	14.54	44	242
07014	Braunschweiger liver sausage pork	2 slices	658	16.16	102	185
07024	Frankfurter, chicken	1	617	8.77	45	116
07069	Salami, beef & pork	2 slices	604	11.40	37	142

Source: USDA

Figure 8.4

Food Content - Lunch - Part III

NSDA #	Food Type	Portion	Mgs Sodium	Grams Fat	Mgs Cholesterol	Calories
21061	Fast food burrito with beans & cheese	1	583	5.85	14	189
21063	Fast food burrito with beans & meat	1	668	8.91	24	254
11533	Tomatoes, red canned	1 cup	564	.48	0	66
21106	Fast food Fish sandwich cheese	1	939	28.60	68	523
21059	Fast food submarine sandwich – shrimp breaded & fried	1	1446	24.90	200	454

Source: USDA

Dinner Food

Dinner was once a time to spend with the family but today it is a time to try and stay alive. Good luck, it is not going to be easy given the content in dinner foods.

If the cholesterol laced egg Mc Muffin you had for breakfast and the sodium packed cheeseburger you had for lunch did not already kill you than I have a dinner line-up that will surely send you to the land beyond.

The death line up starts with fried chicken, a must for any suicide mission. Fried chicken comes packed with 119 mg of cholesterol. Roasted or baked chicken is not much better having 73 mgs of cholesterol. Augment the fried chicken with a side of pork ribs which has 100 mgs of cholesterol or beef ribs with 71 mgs of cholesterol and you are on your way to meet your maker.

If chicken, beef, and pork are full of cholesterol what about turkey or lamb? Well don't look for relief here. Roasted turkey has 106 mgs of cholesterol, almost as much as fried chicken and lamb has 81 mgs of cholesterol.

If land animals are cholesterol storage tanks what about the sea? What about fish? You can cut your cholesterol count by moving from land animals to fish but you are still not out of the woods. Catfish has 69 mgs of cholesterol per 3 oz. Trout has 58 mgs of cholesterol.

To further your meal anguish, try some homemade potato salad. This one shocked me. The DSDA estimates that the innocent looking homemade potato salad, and my one time favorite is a toxic waste land of 1323 mgs of sodium, over 20 grams of fat, 170 mgs of cholesterol and 358 calories. Mom never told me what was in her potato salad and like many moms of her time probably didn't know. If she had known, she would have never served it. Today, you, your mom and anyone else can know what's in the food they prepare and serve by going to the many online web sites that list the ingredients in the food supply. In this book, I am using the USDA-Nutrient Data Laboratory-Agricultural Research Service web site http://www.nal.usda.gov/fnio/foodcomp/.
Once you are on site, click on USDA National Nutrient Database for Standard Reference, Release 16-1.

Listed below (Figure 8.5) are some of the foods that are eaten for dinner and their sodium, fat, cholesterol and calorie content. A complete list can be found on the USDA-Nutrient Data Laboratory-Agricultural Research Service web site. By knowing what is in the food you buy, a person can prepare a healthier meal.

Figure 8.5

<u>Food Content - Dinner - Part I</u>

NSDA #	Food Type	Portion	Sodium Mgs	Fat Grams	Cholesterol Mgs	Calories
05058	Fried Chicken		385	18.48	119	364
05277	Chicken canned	5 oz	714	11.29	88	234
05064	Chicken, roasted	½ breast	64	3.07	73	142
10075	Pork	3 oz	75	19.74	93	280
10193	Pork, back ribs	3 oz	86	25.14	100	315
10153	Pork, cured ham		1128	4.68	47	133
23573	Beef, ground 80% lean 20% fat	3 oz	64	15.15	77	230
13073	Beef ribs	3 oz	54	24.66	71	304
22905	Beef stew, canned	1 cup	947	12.48	37	218
22401	Spaghetti with meat sauce	1 cup	473	2.86	17	255
05168	Turkey, cooked, roasted	1 cup	98	6.96	106	238
05286	Turkey & gravy frozen	5 oz	787	3.73	26	95
17027	Lamb	3 0z	71	8.27	81	184
15119	Fish, Tuna	3 oz	301	6.98	15	168

Source: USDA

Figure 8.5

Food Content – Dinner – Part II

NSDA #	Food Type	Portion	Sodium Mgs	Fat Grams	Cholesterol Mgs	Calories
15084	Fish, Salmon pink canned	3 oz	471	5.14	47	118
15241	Fish, Trout	3 oz	36	6.12	58	144
15034	Fish, Haddock	3 oz	74	.79	63	95
15011	Fish, Catfish	3 oz	238	11.33	69	195
11414	Potato salad, home made		1323	20.50	170	358
11659	Sweet potatoes, home made	1	74	3.41	8	144
11174	Corn, sweet, canned, cream style	1 cup	730	1.08	0	184
20045	Rice, white long grain, regular		2	.44	0	205
11439	Sauerkraut, canned	1 cup	1560	.33	0	45
11549	Tomato products, canned	1 cup	1284	.59	0	78

Source: USDA

Figure 8.5

Food Content – Dinner – Part III

NSDA #	Food Type	Portion	Mgs Sodium	Grams Fat	Mgs Cholesterol	Calories
11569	Turnip greens, without salt	1 cup	42	.33	0	29
11090	Brussels sprouts	1 cup	33	.78	0	56
11090	Broccoli raw	1 cup	29	.11	0	11
11138	Cauliflower, frozen, without salt	1 cup	32	.40	0	34
11575	Turnips, without salt	1 cup	25	.69	0	48
11271	Mustard greens, without salt	1 cup	22	.34	0	21
11114	Cabbage red raw	1 cup	19	.07	0	19

Source: USDA

Dessert - Food

Dessert is one of the world's greatest temptations. Pecan and cherry pies, chocolates and ice cream, all the players you need to end the day dead or at least packed full of enough sodium, fat, cholesterol and calories to live a short and unhealthy life. What has the American diet come to?

All I can say, if you have been eating eggs for breakfast, cheeseburgers for lunch, fried chicken for dinner, you are already on the edge and dessert might be your Waterloo. You can continue on with an unhealthy dessert or pull back from the brink and choose a dessert that is low in cholesterol but high in taste, i.e. frozen yogurt vanilla with 63 mgs of sodium, 4 grams of fat, 1 mg of cholesterol and 117 calories.

How you live is up to you. See a complete list of desserts, the good and bad on the NSDA web page.

Figure 8.6

Dessert

NSDA #	Food Type	Portion	Mgs Sodium	Grams Fat	Mgs Cholesterol	Calories
18336	Pie crust	1 pie shell	976	62.28	0	949
18324	Pie, Pecan, commercial	1 piece	479	20.91	36	452
18325	Pie, Pecan, prepared from recipe	1 piece	320	27.08	106	503
18444	Pie, Fried, cherry	1 piece	479	20.61	0	404
18119	Cake, pineapple upside down	1 piece	367	13.92	25	367
18257	Éclairs filled with chocolates		337	15.70	127	262
18248	Doughnuts, plain	1	76	10.76	17	198
19095	Ice cream, vanilla	½ cup	53	7.26	29	133
19270	Ice Cream, chocolate	½ cup	50	7.26	22	143
19293	Frozen Yogurt vanilla	½ cup	63	4.03	1	117
01057	Eggnog	1 cup	137	19.00	150	343

Source: USDA

Snack – Food

Watch out for those snack foods. They can make your blood pressure go up faster than the game you might be watching. Just 10 pretzels carry a punch of 1029 mgs of sodium. See (Figure 8.7) below. Throw in some cheese covered nachos and you add another 816 mgs of sodium. At this rate, you will be half dead before half time. There are some better snacks that will carry you through the game or party, see the USDA web page.

Figure 8.7

Snack Foods

NSDA #	Food Type	Portion	Mgs Sodium	Grams Fat	Mgs Cholesterol	Calories
19047	Pretzels, salted, plain	10 pretzels	1029	2.10	0	229
11937	Pickles	1	833	.12	0	12
21078	Fast food, nachos with cheese	6-8 nachos	816	18.95	18	346
12635	Nuts with salt	1 oz	190	14.59	0	168
12632	Nuts, macadamia	10-12 nuts	75	21.57	0	203
19410	Potato chips	1oz	186	10.89	18	346
19035	Popcorn oil-popped	1cup	97	3.09	0	55
19108	Jelly beans	10 large	14	.01	0	106

Source: USDA

It seems that water is the healthiest beverage you can consume, see (Figure 8.8) below. It has very little sodium and no fat, cholesterol or calories. It is cheap and natural. Bottle water is also low in sodium and free of fat, cholesterol and calories. Alcohol is also free of most of the bad things but I do not recommend it because of the social cost associated with it, see later Chapter 15 on drinking. A complete list of beverages can be found on the USDA wed site.

Figure 8.8

Beverage

NSDA #	Food Type	Portion	Mgs Sodium	Grams Fat	Mgs Cholesterol	Calories
14006	Alcohol, beer light	12floz	11	0	0	99
14003	Alcohol beer regular	12floz	14	.21	0	117
14400	Carbonated cola, caffeine	8floz	24	0	0	5
14376	Tea, instant	8floz	24	0	0	5
14210	Coffee, espresso, restaurant		8	1.35	0	5
14215	Coffee, instant, regular		4	0	0	4
01111	Milk shake, thick vanilla	11floz	297	9.48	38	351
14429	Water, municipal	8floz	5	0	0	0

Source: USDA

What's for Dinner? How much will it cost me?

Chicken, beef, pork, turkey, lamb and to some degree fish have high concentrations of cholesterol. Vegetables and fruit have a low concentration of cholesterol. If you are going to eat meat and fish then it should be in small amounts and should become less a part of your daily menu. Vegetables on the other hand should become a larger part of your dinning experience. Based on what you choose will determine how long you live and what your health will be. A long and healthy life will give you the opportunity to accomplish your goals. An unhealthy life style could shorten your life preventing you from achieving your goals or supporting your family. In addition, an unhealthy diet can create health problems, requiring costly medical treatment to you and your family. How much will dinner cost? It could be your life and your fortune. It all depends on how you choose.

Friends and Enemies:

Beware of groups, companies and individuals that should have your best interest in mind but could be driven by incentives that benefit them at your expense.

Be aware of Black individuals and companies that advertise products that are unhealthy, unproductive and could prevent you from achieving good health.

You have all been exposed to them. Campbell's Chunky soup has over 1000 milligrams of sodium per serving. High sodium is one of the main causes of strokes, high blood pressure and heart attacks in the Black community yet a high profile Black football player and his mother appears on national television to promote this dangerous product. Also, in Black magazines like Jet and Ebony, cigarettes and alcohol are promoted, even though these products have had devastating impact on the Black community. It seems that for these companies, profits are more important than your life.

Do not think that because someone may have your same skin color that person is interested in your best welfare. Look at each individual, company and product carefully to determine if their products will help you achieve a healthy life style.

Protect Yourself

Most of the food industry is not your friend. If they were your friends, they would not sell products that are harmful to you. They often add unhealthy ingredients to their product just to extend its shelf life. Also, if they were your friend, they would not advertise products that are particular dangers to Black people like Campbell's Chunky Beef soup or KFC's Fried Chicken's fried chicken both with 1000 mgs of sodium per serving. At one time the same company that owned a tobacco company Philip Morris (Altria) also owned a food company (Kraft Foods). You don't know which one will kill you first, the tobacco company or the food company. It is up to you to protect yourself from these companies and their unhealthy products.

Where are the healthy places to eat out?

Finding healthy restaurants is not easy. For the most part, the ingredients in the food served in restaurants seems to be a trade secret and probably for good reason. If you knew what you were eating, you would probably not go out to eat. There are some web sites that list what is in restaurant food. One is called (Chowbaby.com). If you go to their Fast Food Calorie site and select a company, the sodium, fat, cholesterol and calories in each menu is listed.

More healthy restaurants are needed in the Black community. Currently, the Black and poor communities are inundated with unhealthy restaurants like KFC, Burger King, McDonalds, and Wendy's who feed on the ignorance of the poor. They peddle their unhealthy products filled with high amounts of sodium, fat cholesterol and calories, which are the types of food an already overweight Black community does not need.

I have had some success with salad buffet type restaurants like Sweet Tomatoes and Fresh Choice. They have a selection of salads and vegetables and low calorie desserts.

Health cost is going through the roof

Eating the right kinds of food is important to everyone's health and to their pocket book. Following a poor diet is causing heath cost to increase so much that some companies will not hire people who smoke because of the related health cost. This practice will probably grow. Also, at some point a company probably will not pay for employee health cost if the employee is following an unhealthy diet. After all why should they pay for unhealthy eating habits? In the future, people with poor diets may have to pay more for their health insurance versus those that following a healthy life style. Government health care programs like Medicare may also start charging a person based on their eating and smoking habits. Many health problems are preventable and there is no reason why companies or the government should have to pay for medical cost that is caused by a person's choice of how they live. Individuals who follow a healthy life style and do not get sick should not have to pay for those who eat unhealthy food and become sick. Life insurance companies follow this practice today by not paying off an insurance policy if the person takes their own life.

The nation can greatly reduce the cost of Medicare by requiring its members to follow a healthy diet. This would encourage the nation to eat healthier because if you do not follow a health life style, you run the risk of losing their health coverage.

Federal Law requiring Disclosure of Food Content in Restaurants has been passed

Just as the Federal Government requires food labeling on the food you buy at the grocery store, the restaurant business as of January, 2011 is required to list the amount of sodium, fat, cholesterol and calories in the food that they serve. This way a person can make an informed decision on what food to eat. By arming the restaurant goers with information on what not to eat, the health of the nation would be greatly improved and the health cost greatly reduced. Also, restaurants will be encouraged to offer a healthier menu.

This federal law needs to be strengthened. Currently the law only covers businesses with nineteen locations or more.

The law should be strengthened to include any business or organization that sells or gives away food and require them to list the amount of sodium, fat, cholesterol, calories and sugar in their food. After all, you can eat as much unhealthy food at a business with one location as you can with a business with nineteen locations.

Health cost is out of control and we must not lose any opportunity to reduce the cost of health coverage and at the same time save Medicare.

Learn How to Live a Healthy Life

It is worth your time to learn as much about your health and your family's health as possible in order to insure a long and healthy life. What you eat will determine how healthy you live, how long you live and what it will cost you health wise to live. Information on your health is everywhere. The Internet covers most health issues. Whether you have access to the Internet at your home, office or the public library, the information is there. Also, doctors and health professionals like dietitians can provide you and your family with a diet that can provide a healthy and enjoyable dinning experience.

Summary of Chapter 8 - Health & Food

1) Due to unhealthy eating habits, African Americans have one of the highest mortality rates in the country.
2) Read the nutrition facts label on the products you buy. Know what is in the food you eat. It can save your life.
3) Do not eat food high in fat, sodium, calories and cholesterol. This type of food can cause heart attacks, strokes, diabetes, and obesity.
4) Beef, pork, chicken, lamb, turkey and fish have high levels of cholesterol, which can cause heart attacks and strokes. Their consumption should not be the main course of your meal.
5) Vegetables and fruit have little to no amounts of sodium, fat, cholesterol and calories and should be a larger part of your meal.
6) Follow the recommended calories per day which basely is 1600 a day for children, 2200 for active women and most men, and 2,800 for teen boys and active men. This will help you maintain a normal weight.

7) Protect yourself. Don't expect the food industry to look after your health. Most of them are in it for the profits.
8) Future health cost may depend on what condition you are in.
9) The Federal government has passed a national law that requires restaurants to disclose the amount of sodium, fat, cholesterol and calories in the food they service.

Chapter 9 – Health & Obesity

People who are overweight will die sooner than people who are slim.

Overweight & Obesity is Hazardous to your Health

Many obesity-related diseases including diabetes, hypertension, cancer and heart disease are found in higher rates among Blacks, per the CDC. Listed below are some of the health hazards associated with being overweight or obese.

1) Obesity is associated with a higher risk of colon, breast and perhaps other cancers, according to the American Institute of Cancer Research.
2) Obesity appears to contribute to the higher risk of pancreatic cancer among black Americans, particularly for women per CDC.
3) Being overweight accounts for up to a third of all cases of cancer.
4) Among African Americans, the high rate of obesity and obesity-related conditions such as hypertension and type 2 diabetes, are contributing to a high rate of death from coronary heart disease, per CDC.
5) The high rate of obesity in the Black community is contributing to the high rate of hypertension in the Black population, per CDC.
6) Diabetes has been reported to occur at a rate of 16 to 26 percent in Hispanic Americans and black Americans, aged 45 to 74. This compares with 12 percent in whites (non-Hispanic) of the same age.

Overweight & Obesity is Growing Among Blacks

Nearly eighty percent of the Black female population of the United States is overweight.

Overweight and obesity is growing out of control in the Black community. The percentage of overweight Blacks have gone from 62.5 in 1994 to 75.5 in 2008. The percentage of obese Blacks have increased from 30.2 in 1994 to 44.3 in 2008, see (Figure 9.1) below. Nearly eighty percent of the Black female population of the United States is overweight and over seventy percent of the Black male population is overweight, see (figure 9.2) below.

Figure 9.1

Increase in Overweight and Obesity from 1988 to 2008 by Race

Race	Overweight 1988 to 1994	Overweight 1999 to 2000	Overweight 2005 to 2008	Obesity 1988 to 1994	Obesity 1999 to 2000	Obesity 2005 to 2008
Black	62.5 %	69.6 %	75.5%	30.2 %	39.9 %	44.3%
Mexican American	67.4 %	73.4 %	77.4%	28.4%	34.4 %	36.7%
White	52.6 %	62.3 %	66.5%	21.2 %	28.7 %	32.9%

Source: CDC, National Center for Health Statistics, National Health & Nutrition Examination Survey

Figure 9.2

Increase in Overweight Men and Women from 1988 to 2008 (percentage)

Race	Men 1988 to 1994	Men 1999 to 2000	Men 2005 to 2008	Women 1988 to 1994	Women 1999 to 2000	Women 2005 to 2008
Black	58.2	60.1	71.1	68.5	78	78
Mexican American	69.4	74.4	75.3	69.6	71.8	72.3
White	61.6	67.5	72.9	47.2	57.5	59.6

Source: CDC, National Center for Health Statistics, National Health & Nutrition Examination Survey

Obesity and Competition

The writers of the Ebony magazine March, 2000 article, "Why so Many Black Women are Overweight," stated health as the reason why obesity is bad for Black women. Another reason why being overweight is bad for Black women is that it is unattractive, although, some women in the Black community perceive obesity as a virtue, or at least, not a problem. In comparison, most of the women outside of the Black community see obesity as unappealing and are doing everything they can to prevent being overweight. We live in a competitive world and when competing for a soul mate, the women with the most attractive package will have the upper hand. In the old days, it was a dowry. Today it is looks, kindness and education. Black women have the kindness, and are gaining the education, but they will need to exercise and eat healthy to keep the weight off in order to maintain an attractive look. The results will be a healthier and stronger Black family and a more attractive and competitive Black woman.

Obesity and Discipline

Obesity in the Black community seems be the result of a lack of discipline and health education. Discipline is needed to stay away from fatty foods. I once knew a girl who refused to stop eating fried chicken. The fried chicken along with a cupboard full of other fatty foods had made her obese, but for some reason she did not connect the fact that what you eat is what you will become. Also, she did not connect obesity with diabetes, heart failure and high blood pressure, which often leads to a shorter life span. Besides the health issues, she also did not connect obesity to a person being a social outcast, unattractive, and often unmarried.

In the past, being overweight was not acceptable. Then, the word was, no one likes a fat person. Today in the Black community being overweight seems to be acceptable. Accepting obesity is like accepting something that will give you poor health, less social avenues and a shorter life expectancy.

Also, obesity has torn at the social fabric of the Black community. Few men in our society would choose to marry an obese woman over a woman whose weight compliments her body. The prettier a woman is the more likely she will find a soul mate. Also, in our society, it often takes two incomes to support a family. See Family Planning Chapter 11 (Figure 11.1) on single-family income vs. two income families. Obesity has destabilized the family by making the married female less attractive to her mate, which in turn makes other females who are not overweight more attractive to her husband.

A Simple Observation

Often I ride my bike down the trail near my home in northern California. These trips are enlightening and discouraging. The trail is full of people of all races and nationalities. The one constant is that the Asian women are small and thin and the Black women are large and overweight, really over weight.
Usually the Asian women are running and the Black women are just barely walking down the trail. This observation can be seen in almost every town in America where there are Black women. What has happened to the Black women as far as their appearance? When I was in school during the 1960s, obesity was rare and not acceptable. Now almost every Black woman in the country is overweight. I believe that obesity in the Black community is because of a lack of discipline. I see this in three parts. Part one is an unwillingness to learn what foods not to eat and part two, an unwillingness to stop eating the type and quantity of food that causes obesity. Part three is a lack of exercise.

I did not have to go far to see this unwillingness to change. A few years ago, I approached a friend about the type of food she was preparing for her family. You would have thought that I was asking for the ingredients to an atom bomb. She defended the type of food she serviced with the determination of a caged lion. I believe that her reaction can probably be repeated in millions of Black households throughout the nation. Recipes handed down from grandmother to mother to daughter are the equivalence of the family shield or family charter. Often these recipes are laden with fat, sodium and cholesterol, which are the ingredients for obesity. Add the fast food restaurants and the lack of exercise and you have an unhealthy and overweight Black population, and all of the negatives that go along with it.

When are you overweight or obese?

See (Figure 9.3) below from the Department of Health & Human Services (HHS) and the Department of Agriculture (USDA) of a healthy weight, overweight, or obese person. It is only a guideline but can give you some idea as to where your

weight falls in the healthy and not so healthy range. Personally, I feel that the government is being generous with the amount of weight they consider a healthy weight. A person 5'5" according to the chart can weight up to 150 and still be considered to have a healthy weight even though, one pound over that and you fall into the overweight category. I would want to stay at the low to middle range of the healthy weight category to be safe. Also, when it comes to weight, you should think of what is healthy first but do not forget looks. It matters how you look. Few people look good carrying excess weight.

Figure 9.3

<u>Healthy Weight, Overweight & Obesity</u>

Height	Healthy Weight	Overweight	Obesity
6'6"	165-220	221-260	261-275
6'5"	160-210	211-255	256-275
6'4"	155-205	206-250	251-275
6'3"	150-200	201-240	421-275
6'2"	145-190	191-235	236-275
6'1"	143-185	186-230	231-275
6'0"	140-180	181-220	221-275
5'11"	135-175	176-215	216-275
5'10"	130-173	174-210	211-275
5'9"	125-170	171-205	206-275
5'8"	120-165	166-200	201-275
5'7"	115-160	161-190	191-275
5'6"	113-155	156-185	186-275
5'5"	111-150	151-180	181-275
5'4"	110-145	146-175	176-275
5'3"	105-140	141-170	171-275
5'2"	102-135	136-165	166-275
5'1"	99-130	131-160	161-275
5'0"	95-125	126-155	156-275
4'11"	90-123	124-150	151-275
4'10"	85-120	121-145	146-275

Source: Department of Health & Human Services (HHS) & Department of Agriculture (USDA), Nutrition & Your Health, Dietary Guidelines for Americans

Body Mass Index (BMI)

Obesity is defined as having a body-mass index of 30 or above. The index is a measure of weight relative to height. Healthy weight is a BMI of less than 25.

Body mass index (BMI) is measure of body fat based on height and weight that applies to both adult men and women.

BMI Categories:

- Underweight = <18.5
- Normal weight = 18.5-24.9
- Overweight = 25-29.9
- Obesity = BMI of 30 or greater

To determine your BMI, locate one of the many BMI calculators on the Internet. Enter your weight and height and the calculator will do the rest. The National Institute of Health, a part of the Department of Health & Human Services also has a BMI calculator on their web site: (www.nhlbisupport.com/bmi/bmicalc.htm). In addition, they have a menu planner. With the planner, you can plan the number of calories you and your family consumes which allows you to control your BMI or weight. Your goal should be to maintain a normal weight.

Exercise

A sedentary life style can contribute to obesity. Black people are not exercising enough and need to get out there and become more active in sports and other activity that exercises the body. As the old saying goes, you use it or lose it. Well of late, we have been losing it. My personal choice of exercising is running or biking. I am doing more of the biking now because after running two marathons in my fifties, my body does not seem to want to run the 60 miles a week that is required to train for a marathon. For those who want the challenge of a lifetime, there is nothing like a 26.2-mile marathon. By the way, some of the winners of the major marathons run 200 miles a week in training. Now that is dedication. Also, it is not so important how far or long you run, bike, swim, and lift weights.

What is important is that you exercise on regular basis and that the workout is enough to maintain a healthy body weight. Exercise is a lifetime endeavor.

Summary of Chapter 9 - Health & Obesity

1) Many obesity-related diseases including diabetes, hypertension, cancer and heart disease are found in higher rates among Blacks.
2) Nearly eighty percent of the Black female population of the United States is overweight.
3) Maintain a BMI of less than 25 for a healthy body weight.
4) Plan your own health by using a meal planner.
5) Exercise regularly. It could be the difference between life and death.

Chapter 10 – Marriage

One of the most important decisions you will make in your life will be whom you marry.

Marriage

Getting married or not getting married. Who to marry? When to marry? Having children or not having children. If children, when? These are some of the most important questions a person will face in their lifetime. How these questions are addressed will determine the quality of your life.

It has been said that you can love a rich man as well as a poor man. I suggest that if you marry a rich man or woman, work to keep them rich and if you marry a poor man or woman, work to make them rich.

Know whom you are Dating and whom you are Marrying

When I first met my wife, she put me through a series of questions. This did not happen on the first date, this happened on the first time I saw her. The questions were basic like, are you married, do you have a job, and do you have a car.

I did not think much of it at the time but I was being interviewed for a possible lifetime relationship. I managed to pass this first series of test but as I found out later, this was only the beginning and that a more detailed investigation was to follow. Who you date and marry is one of the most important decisions of your life. Your mate will help determine your standard of living, the size of your family, the level of your happiness, your career, the location of where you live in the country or out of the country, what your kids will look like, their health, size, IQ and countless other large and small things.

Marriage is for Life or should be

Question your Date

How often do you hear from a divorcee, I did not really know my husband or wife? I did not know that he had a drinking problem or that she could not bear children. The time to find out about whom you are dating is immediate.

Listed below in (Figure 10.1) is a questionnaire on how to know your date and how to rate them.

Figure 10.1

Questionnaire on Getting to Know a Potential Soul Mate Part I

Questions	Cause and Effect
Are you married?	If the person is married then you would want to know why he or she is not with their spouse.
Are you in a serious relationship?	If not married but it could be so close to it that it is not worth your time or effort.
Do you have a job?	Work is essential. A person without a job can be more a detriment than a benefit.
What type of work do you do?	Look for a person with potential. The type of job a person does is a reflection of who that person is.
Is marriage in your future?	If you are looking for marriage and he or she is not, that should be known up front.
Is this a serious relationship?	Know the ground rules up front.
Do you believe in dating exclusively?	This will let you know where you stand.
What is your sex drive?	If yours is low and his is high that may be grounds for infidelity.
What is your education level?	In general, the more a person is educated the more money that person will make in their lifetime.
What activities do you like?	What do you have in common? Most men like sports, most women do not but there are other things like dinning, movies, traveling that both enjoy.
How much TV do you watch?	If a man is watching sports all the time and a woman is watching the soaps all the time then determine if a compromise can be worked out.

Figure 10.1

<u>Questionnaire on Getting to Know a Potential Soul Mate Part II</u>

Questions	Cause and Effect
What are your goals?	For some people who have had to fight poverty all of their lives it may not be easy to see beyond the next low paying job but it is essential that you do. It is not where you are but where you are going.
Do you want children?	You should know up front.
Are you capable of producing or having children?	If not, why not?
What do you think about adopting children?	Do not let this be a surprise later on.
Do you have children?	If so, will the children live with you? If they will live with you, can you handle it?
Do you have a criminal record?	A person's criminal past could affect that person's ability to get a job and if it was a violent crime, there could be a safety issue. Determine if the criminal record is a date breaker. Often a person with little education will have a criminal record because that is the only way that person can make a living. Also, a person may lie about their past and some research on your part may be necessary such as going on-line to some of the services that can investigate criminal records.
Were you married before?	If so, what happened? Try and determine if what happened before could happen again.

Figure 10.1

Questionnaire on Getting to Know a Potential Soul Mate Part III

Questions	Cause and Effect
Do you use legal drugs?	If there is a heavy drug use there must be a serious medical problem.
Do you use illegal drugs?	If a person has a drug problem, look out. A drug addiction can drain a person's finances, lead to delusion and depression and a miserable relationship.
Do you or have you ever had aids or other venereal diseases?	This is a life and death question and requires an answer that you can trust. Be assured of the answer and back that up with protection. Your health is the most important thing you have and you must protect it at all times.
What relationship would you maintain once you are married?	Is it necessary for the boys to always be over to the house? Does the night out with the boys continue?
Would any of your parents or other family members live with you if you got married?	Marriage is very personal; know whom you will be living with.
Will your job require you to be out of town?	Pilots, flight attendants, over the road sales people, professional sports people may be away from home fifty percent of the time. Can you handle this type of living?
Do you drink alcohol?	Alcoholism is a major problem for the family. In some cases, it will have negative effects on a person and the family. The best way to avoid alcoholism is to be with someone who does not drink.

Figure 10.1

Questionnaire on Getting to Know a Potential Soul Mate Part IV

Questions	Cause and Effect
Do you smoke?	Smoking is addictive and a serious health problem. Smokers are controlled by their addiction, which could come first in their lives. In many cases, the smoke will lead to the poor health and early death of the smoker and in some cases, the second hand smoke will cause serious health problem for the spouse and other family members.
Are you heterosexual?	Need to know.
What is your credit rating?	A responsible person has good credit. Without good credit, your ability to generate assets is limited. With good credit, loans for homes, businesses, and low interest credit cards are available.
Do you maintain a diet?	You are what you eat and too many French fries, burgers and chocolates will show up in the form of obesity, heart attacks, high blood pressure and other health problems.
How important is religion to you? Do you believe in marriage outside your religion?	I grow up in a religion diverse home and never knew it because my parents respected each other's religion and never made religion a battleground. Some religions require both parents and their kids to observe the same religion. Both couples in a relationship should know religion requirements.

Figure 10.1

Questionnaire on Getting to Know a Potential Soul Mate Part V

Questions	Cause and Effect
How does the person handle their finances?	Do they bounce checks? Are creditors always calling? Has their car been repossessed? Do they pay for small amounts with a credit card because they do not have the money? Will retailers accept their checks?
Parent test	What will he or she look like in twenty years, just look at the parents? Unless there is a change in life style, the children will look like their parents in about twenty years.

Now I am not suggesting that you have a clipboard and an interview on your first date. These are questions to be worked in over dinner or long walks.

Marriage and Resources

Money and other assets will make your life a lot easier. By knowing the direction you want to go, you can plan resources to get there. Money will be one of the major requirements of a family. When to start a family will be another. Today it takes ten of thousands of dollars to bring up a child. Money will be needed for prenatal care, pre-school, after school activities, medical, housing, clothing and colleges just to name some of the major cost.

You can help ensure that the money will be there by employing the following recommendations:

Education First then Marriage

Getting married and raising a family is costly. It is important for a man and a woman to have an education in order to hold down a job or start and run a business. In the past, a man worked and a woman stayed at home and raised

the family. Today with the high cost of living it often takes both the husband and the wife working to meet the daily expenses and save for college and investments. Also, there is a high rate of divorces in the country, and a woman needs to be just as prepared as a man to support the family. The U.S. Census Bureau in 2002 estimated that the divorce rate was around 50%.

Getting an education when a person is young is a lot easier than waiting until after a family has been started. Minimum education should be a college degree. At one time, a high school diploma was the minimum, but advancing technology has all but eliminated jobs that require only a high school diploma. A college degree will give a person the foundation for dealing with today's changing world. Even those persons not going on to advance degrees, will need a college education to communicate in a changing and increasingly global market place. For example, truck drivers will need to know how domestic and foreign markets affect their loads, licensing and wage structure. They may not only drive the truck, but may want to buy the trucking company and run it. This will require negotiating and business skills, which can be learned in a Business College.

A solid education will lay the foundation to a solid career or business. It is important that the educational process take priority over marriage. Education comes first, then marriage and family.

Once Married, have Children when You can
Afford to

You have probably heard the saying that you can always feed one more mouth. When the United States was an agrarian society and a new member to the family meant an additional farm hand this may have been true. Today most families do not live on farms and an addition to the family represents an added cost for housing, education and medical coverage. One additional child could push the family into financial instability.

Children are for life, so be prepared to support them for the rest of your life. Support would include college cost, down payment on their first home and estate planning and inheritance.

College Cost

My parents never provided any money for my college education, either because they could not or would not. I am not sure. My father did get me a job at his company. It was a low paying job but the income was enough to allow me to start college at night. Also, I was lucky because back in the 60s, we still had manufacturing jobs that paid good union wages. With the union job, I made enough in the summer to attend college full time through the school year. Today many of these jobs are countries away but still someone must pay the cost of college. I believe that when a couple brings a child into the world, they are responsible for that child's education up to and including college.

Fifty years ago, having a high school diploma could get you a good paying job. This is not the case today. Today, a four-year college degree is required to get most good paying jobs. Also, back then and to some extent today, many parents felt that once their children reached eighteen, they were on their own. Times have changed. Today, a parent is required to support their child through the age of twenty-two or through college.

Down Payment on Their First Home

Should a parent help their children with the down payment on their first home? My father never gave me any money for a home so I was inclined not to give money to my children.

I was brought up with the belief that you worked for what you get and I still believe in it but maybe I should also look at what the more prosperous groups of our society are doing.

Many of the more well to do groups in our society do give money to their children when the child is starting a family.

By the parent giving their offspring a down payment on a home, the child immediately starts to build equity. The equity can then be used to buy another home, normally larger and in a better neighborhood, with better schools that provide a better education for their children. These better-educated children then get better jobs and can then buy a better home. This process allows the child to be even better or richer than the parent as each generation moves upward. Also, the homes are providing tax deductions and collateral for loans that can be used to start businesses and make more money. If you think that giving money to your children is going to produce positive results then by all means do so.

Estate Planning and Inheritance

Build wealth in the Black community through estate planning. You cannot take it with you so why not pass the money on to your kids so that they do not have to start the process of wealth building all over again. Blacks can acquire wealth by each generation building on the previous generation. Also by effective estate planning, you can reduce estate taxes and leave more to your family. Wills, trust and other estate planning documents should be in place well before your departure. Consult your attorney and the Internet for information on estate planning.

One-Income vs. Two-Income Families

It is easier for a two-income family to bring up a child than a one-income family. The United States and perhaps most of the world is driven by money. Some people work fifteen-hour days to earn money and some simply inherit it. In some families, all the members of the family work for the family business as in a small grocery store. Some families have one person making big money and some families have many family members making low wages that can add up to big money.

In most Black families, more than one member of the family will have to work in order for the family to prosper financially.

What is important is that they pool their resources and apply them toward goals that are mutually beneficial to the whole family.

Two-incomes, three-incomes or the whole family working together is a prescription for success.

<u>Summary of Chapter 10 – Marriage</u>

1) One of the most important decisions you will make in your life will be whom you marry.
2) Know whom you are marrying.
3) Get married after you have completed your education. You will need the money.
4) Once married, have children when you can afford to.
5) It is easier for a two-income family to bring up a child than a one-income family.

Chapter 11 – Family Planning

Do not have Children before Marriage

The percentage of Black children in poverty in single-mother families is 50.2%

See (Figure 11.1) below on the percentage of Black children in poverty. This says that more than half of the Black children who live with unmarried parents will live in poverty. This is a condition that should be avoided at all cost. This compares with the percentage of Black children in poverty that live with married parents at 11% or a little more than the national average of 8.5%.

Married or not married, if you are the parent of a child it is your responsibility to love and provide for that child.

Figure 11.1

Percentage of Children in Poverty

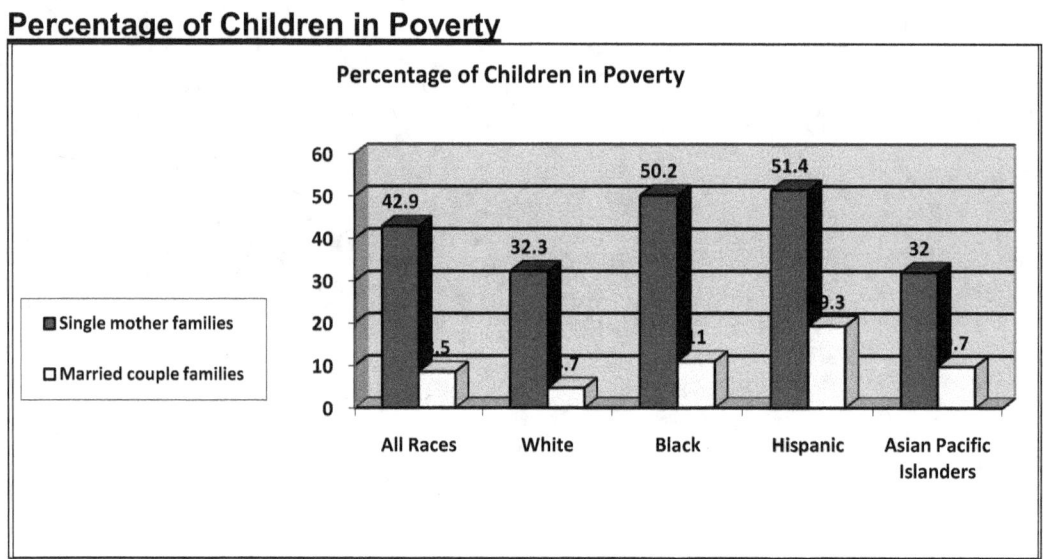

Source: US Census Bureau. Annual Social and Economic Supplement, March 2008

Statistics show that most unmarried Black women, who get pregnant, are left by the father of the child.

How not to have Unplanned Children

A) Abstention from intercourse. Easier say than done for some but do not let your sex drive or wanting to be accepted dictate your life. One sex partner on one occasion can put you into poverty for the rest of your life. Do not let this happen to you. Just say no.

B) If abstention is not working and intercourse is desired, keep in mind that intercourse is the exchange of bodily fluids and is designed to produce life. If you do not want life than you had better place a barrier between you and the person you are having intercourse with. Also, with the **Aids** virus traveling in seamen from the male to the female, intercourse could mean death; see (Figure 11.2 & 11.3) below on the HIV infection rate. The most common used barrier is a condom. Condoms can prevent the spread of Aids. This is the minimum protection against pregnancy and venereal diseases. If you are not absolutely sure about your sexual partner's medical history, never have sex without a condom. In the Black community, Black males will often eschew the condom but it is up to the women to protect her life. Women should not let anyone take her life away by not protecting herself. Also, statistics show that most unmarried Black woman who get pregnant, are left by the father of the child.

Sexual Transmitted Diseases

Blacks have the highest rate of death from HIV than any group in the nation.

One of the biggest killers of Black people is HIV. Although Blacks make up 12 percent of the population they are more likely to be diagnoses with HIV than any other race in the country. The HIV rate for Black men in 2007 was 24.5 per 100,000 residents see (Figure 11.2). This rate is over six times the national rate. The rate for Black women was 11.3 per 100,000 residents see (Figure 11.3). This rate is 16 times the rate for White women. Figure 11.4 gives an estimated of adult and adolescent HIV and AIDS diagnoses in 2008, by race/ethnicity.

Transmission Route of AIDS

Figure 11.5 and figure 11.6 identify the transmission route of AIDS. Knowing how AIDS is transmitted is the first line of defends against the disease.

Figure 11.2

Male Death Rate for HIV (per 100,000 residents population)

Race	1987	1990	1995	1998	1999	2000	2001	2007
All Races	5.6	10.2	16.2	5.6	5.3	5.2	5.0	3.7
White	8.7	15.7	20.4	5.2	4.9	4.6	4.4	3.1
Black	26.2	46.3	89.0	38.0	36.1	35.1	33.8	24.5
Hispanic	18.8	28.8	40.8	11.7	10.9	10.6	9.7	6.3
American Indian or Alaska Native	N/a	3.3	10.5	4.0	4.2	3.5	4.2	3.6
Asian or Pacific Islander	2.5	4.3	6.0	1.5	1.4	1.2	1.2	0.8

Source: NCHS

Figure 11.3

Female Death Rate for HIV (per 100,000 residents population)

Race	1987	1990	1995	1998	1999	2000	2001	2007
White	0.6	1.1	2.5	0.9	1.0	1.0	0.9	0.7
Black	4.6	10.1	24.4	13.7	13.1	13.2	13.4	11.3
Hispanic	2.1	3.8	8.8	3.2	3.0	2.9	2.7	1.8
American Indian or Alaska Native	N/A	N/A	2.5	N/A	1.0	1.0	N/A	1.7
Asian or Pacific Islander	N/A	N/A	0.6	N/A	0.2	0.2	N/A	N/A

Source: NCHS

Figure 11.4

Estimated adult and adolescent HIV and AIDS diagnoses in 2008, by race/ethnicity

Race/ethnicity	HIV Men	HIV Women	HIV Total	AIDS Men	AIDS Women	AIDS Total
White	9918	1833	11783	8981	1583	10571
Black	14283	6907	21312	11974	6341	18341
Hispanic/ Latino	6557	1681	8260	6240	1619	7864
Asian	363	78	444	430	97	527
American Indian or Alaska Native	167	52	220	155	44	199
Native Hawaiian/ Pacific Islander	30	6	36	48	7	55
Multiple races	277	104	384	310	121	435
Total*	31595	10662	42439	28137	9813	37991

* Values in each column may not sum to the column total, as the column totals for estimated numbers were calculated independently of the values for the subpopulations.

Source: AVERT

Figure 11.5

<u>**Estimated adult and adolescent males living with an AIDS diagnosis in 2007 by race/ethnicity and exposure category**</u>

Transmission Route:

Race/ethnicity	Male-to male sexual contact	Injection drug use	Male-to male sexual contact & drug use	High-risk hetero-sexual contact	Other	Total
White	107544	12236	13013	5165	1717	139676
Black	62124	34603	10946	24861	1054	133588
Hispanic/ Latino	42821	19293	5467	8536	623	76740
Asian	2912	235	186	377	87	3798
American Indian or Alaska Native	756	193	240	83	12	1284
Native Hawaiian/ Pacific Islander	288	14	20	21	2	346
Multiple races	1589	519	315	300	29	2751
Total **	218136	67121	30196	39353	3527	358332

* Because totals are calculated independently of the subpopulations, values in each column may not sum exactly to the figure in the 'Total' column. ** Includes persons of unknown race/ethnicity.

Source: Avert

Figure 11.6

Estimated adult and adolescent females living with an AIDS diagnosis in 2007 by race/ethnicity and exposure category

Transmission Route:

Race/ethnicity	Injection drug use	High-risk hetero-sexual contact	Other	Total
White	7863	11347	586	19796
Black	19877	44007	1382	65267
Hispanic/ Latino	6474	14145	527	21146
Asian	85	594	91	770
American Indian or Alaska Native	159	227	14	400
Native Hawaiian/ Pacific Islander	11	60	6	77
Multiple races	360	689	34	1082
Total **	34845	71088	2643	108576

Source: AVERT

Just as poverty can be the root of all evil, unprotected sex can be the root of death. Blacks have the highest rate of death from HIV than any group in the nation. HIV is a preventable disease, which makes it your choice whether you live or die. Protect yourself at all times so that you do not become a statistic of the NCHS.

Birth Control

There are many organizations that provide service and products to control birth. One is listed below. Other sources of birth control information can be found in the telephone directory, Internet, through private physicians and hospitals, and with friends and family.

Planned Parenthood Federation of America is an organization that provides information on birth control. Their toll free number is 1-800-230-7526. Web address: (www.plannedparenthood.org).
Their web site includes the following information:

Reversible Methods:

1) Behavioral: Abstinence, Predicting fertility, and withdrawal.

2) Barriers: Condoms male and female. Condoms can be effective against pregnancies and sexually transmitted infections including HIV. Other barriers include diaphragms and cervical caps.

3) Hormonal: Included in this group are birth control pills, the Norplant which can last up to five years and the Depo-Provera which can prevent pregnancy up to 12 weeks. Others are the Patch and the Ring.

4) Intrauterine Devices or IUDs is another type of birth control.
5) Emergency Contraception or the morning-after pill is also available.

Permanent Methods (sterilization):
Sterilization for women and Vasectomy for men.

For a complete list of birth control methods contact Planned Parenthood Federation of America.

Adoption

If the birth control methods mentioned above fail and an unwanted pregnancy does occur, the child can be put up for adoption.

Abortions

If all else fails, and an unwanted pregnancy does occur, a women can have an abortion if it is preformed during the first three months of the pregnancy. This is a very tough decision and everything possible should be done so that this decision does not have to be made. Choosing to have an abortion seems to be especially tough in the Black community. Many Black women oppose abortions but it can be the difference between poverty and wealth. As Figure 11.1on poverty above shows, 50.2% of the children of single–mothers live in poverty.

Abortion information

Planned Parenthood Federation of America can provide information for abortions. The toll free number is 1-800-230-7526. Web address: (www.plannedparenthood.org).

Other On-Line Abortion site

333Another site for abortion information is Abortion Clinics On-Line (ACOL). This is a directory service made up of websites of over 400 providers of abortion services and other reproductive healthcare services. They include private physicians, state licensed clinics, private clinics, and hospital abortion services. Abortion clinics listed are in 40 states and international locations.

Abortion Clinics On-Line has been online since 1995 and has had over eight million visitors.

Summary of Chapter 11 – Family Planning

1) Do not have kids before you get married.
2) How not to have unplanned children.
3) Guard against sexually transmitted diseases. One of the biggest killers of Black people is HIV.
4) Use birth controls to prevent unplanned pregnancies.

Chapter 12 – Image and Appearance

For everyone it takes effort to be the best at anything

You will be judged on how you look

Whether for a potential date or a potential job, looks matter. Upon first contact with a person, they will see you before they hear you and will form an opinion. It will be up to how you speak and what you say that will confirm or modify that opinion.

Not every one will be Miss America or Mr. Universe but every one can try to come as close to these models of physical success as possible. Miss America or Mr. Universe may look like they have it all but even these individuals may not have been born with the attributes that won them fame. For example, Miss America probably had to straighten her teeth with braces at a young age or Mr. Universe had to develop muscles through hours of training in the gym. For everyone, it takes effort to be the best at anything.

Know what is Attractive.

What may appear to be attractive in your community may not be attractive in the community you want to go to. Take a look at where you want to be and see how they speak, dress or eat. I can look at my own experience on this subject. I was the first male in my family to go to college. My father, who worked hard at a labor intense job, took a bath once a week. As far as I know, this was the standard so I also took a bath once a week. One of my early college courses was a class in business dress and cleanliness. I was completely shocked when the instructor informed the class that you should take a minimum of one shower or bath a day, preferable in the morning before you come into contact with the outside world.

Up to that point, my world had told me that one shower a week was enough. My information on the number of showers per week was based on where I was and not where I wanted to be. As soon as the class was over, the shower was my next stop.

Your Smile is Important

Your smile is your first greeting card. It is important to present the best first impression and therefore your teeth must be their best. Yellow and broken teeth should be cleaned and repaired. A gap between your two front teeth is not a good first impression. Nor is it a fashion statement as some would claim. This is work for an orthodontist. Another non-fashionable statement is a visible gold tooth. This look may have been acceptable when the West was being won or stolen but today gold teeth should be covered with white porcelain. Teeth should be brushed three times a day for two minutes and flossed once a day. Teeth should also be cleaned and checked twice a year by a dentist. Appearances and image is important for many reasons. You want to make yourself as sellable and presentable as possible to customers, clients, prospective job interviewers, loan officers and future soul mates. There are many jobs that require a good smile. They include flight attendants, public relation jobs and news reporters. These public contact jobs may not be your main interest, but by having a good smile, you do not exclude yourself from these jobs. Attractive teeth will make you more competitive for more jobs.

Dress & Appearance

Look Positive and Professional

One day, I was flipping through the television channels looking for a station that did not portray Blacks as clowns or servants, which is not easy, when I came across an Asian station. I had no idea of what they were saying because they were not speaking English, but never the less, I was impressed with them because of their presentation. Each person on the station whether it was a newsperson, a talk show host or even the people in the ads, were appropriately dressed for the message they were trying to convey. Their presentation was always positive and believable. Even though I could not understand what they were saying, they seem believable because of their manners and appearance. They appeared confident in what they were doing and their dress and manners enforced their believability. Always dress, look, and act in a manner that makes you look confident and believable. It is the first step to getting ahead.

Appearance Makes the Man and the Woman

Some Blacks seem to go out of their way to look anti-social

How you look is important. If you dress like a holdup man, someone is likely to call the cops on you. Blacks seem to go out of their way to look as anti-social as possible. Blacks seem to be trying to draw attention to themselves for all of the wrong reasons. Take for instance the shaved head look on some Black men. For centuries, men have done everything to keep their hair. Why would Black men who can grow a healthy head of hair shave their hair off? Is it to get attention or to do the opposite of what is expected in society or simply to scare people? Whatever the reason, they got what they wanted, the oddball look. Of course, when you look odd you are treated odd and normally that treatment is not very good when it come to jobs, status in the community and treatment by the police or other enforcement agencies. For example, there are few shaved head people hired into corporate America, which is where the jobs are. There are few shaved head people in government, because people do not vote for the odd ball. There are few shaved head people in the legal profession because people do not trust odd-looking judges, lawyers or even juries. If you insist on being the odd ball prepare to be treated badly. Do not expect to be hired into corporate America. Do not expect to practice law. Do not expect to be voted in as the Congressperson or Senator. By looking unsociable you will have eliminated yourself from consideration from nearly the whole job market.

Look and be Professional to get the great job

In order to get the great jobs, make yourself as appealing to society as possible. Always present yourself in a professional manner, which would include the following:

1) Wear the correct hairstyle. Hair should be cut neat and clean and give off the appearance that you are professional and would fit into the organization you are trying to join. Do not wear dreadlocks, braids, do's, or a shaved head.
2) Clothes should look new, modern and reflect the position you seek.
3) Men should not wear earrings and women's earrings should be small.
4) Do not become obese. You will be judged on your physical appearance. The better you look, the better your chances of getting a job.
5) Speak English. Do not speak Ebonics, ghetto language, or slang because they are the language of the uneducated and will give a negative view of who you are.
6) Be on time or early for any job interviews. Show the employer that you are dependable and very interested in the job.
7) Research the company you want to work for. Know who they are and what they produce or what their services are.
8) Be prepared to talk about how you can make a contribution to their company.
9) Before applying for a position, determine what are the education, training and experiences needed to do the job and obtain these requirements through college, trade school or other activities that would make you qualified for a certain position.

Summary of Chapter 12 - Image and Appearance

1) You will be judged on how you look. Look as positive and professional as you can.
2) Know what is attractive. What may be acceptable in the neighborhood you are from may not be acceptable in the neighborhood you want to go to.
3) Attractive teeth will make you more competitive for more jobs.
4) Appearance makes the man and the woman. Dress like you belong.

Chapter 13 - Crime

Nearly a third of all Black men have criminal records

Crime is Destroying the Black Community

The prisons are filled with Blacks. According to the Department of Justice, in June 2009, there were 2,297,400 million inmates in US jails, the highest in the world. Sixty percent or 1,378,440 were members of racial or ethnic minorities. Thirty nine percent of them were Black see Figure 13.1. Their lives, their families, and their communities are suffering because they cannot earn a living to take care of themselves or their families. Even when they get out of prison, their job prospects are limited because they have a criminal record.

A person with a criminal record is excluded from thousands of jobs by law. Thousands of other jobs are also not available in companies that do not hire felons. Add in the fact that a person may not have a high school diploma or a college degree and it is easy to see why so many Blacks are unemployed and why so many Blacks have turned to crime to make a living.

Figure 13.1
Prison Population 2009 by race

Blacks	895,986
Whites	873,012
Hispanics	482,454
Other	45,948
Total	2,297400

Source: Department of Justice

Black Men and Prison

Per the Department of Justice, in 2006, an estimated 12 percent of all black men in their 20's were in jails or prisons. The rate for Latino men was 3.7 percent and the rate for White men was 1.6 percent.

Lifetime chances of a person going to prison are shown in Figure 13.2 below

Figure 13.2
Lifetime chances of a person going to prison by race

Blacks	18.6%
Hispanics	10%
Whites	3.4%

Source: Department of Justice

Over 39% of Jailed inmates are Black

Although Blacks make up about 12% of the US population, in 2008 they were 39% of the jail inmates see (Figure 13.3) below.

Figure 13.3

Local Jail Inmates 1990-2008

Year Race	1990	1995	1997	2000	2001	2005	2008
White	169600	203300	230300	260500	271700	331000	333300
Black	172300	220600	237900	256300	256200	290500	308000
Hispanic	58000	74400	88900	94100	93000	111900	128500
Other	5400	8800	10000	10200	10300	13000	14000
Total	405300	507140	567100	621100	631200	746400	783800

Note: Excludes Federal and State prisons.

Source: U.S. Census Bureau 2011

The United States has become a nation that does not solve problems but jails them and there does not seem to be any national effort to reverse this trend. The total State prison population increased 378,500 from 1990 to 2008. Blacks account for 135,700 of the increase.

With the United States three strikes and you are out laws, which fills up the prisons, and the collapse of the public school system in the inner cities which does not prepare their students for college or trade schools, and the end to affirmative action which attempted to achieve equal job opportunity, many Blacks find themselves headed to prison, in prison, or just released from prison.

Based on current rates of first incarceration, an estimated 32% of black males will enter State or Federal prison during their lifetime, compared to 17% of Hispanic males and 5.9% of white males.
Sources: Department of Justice/BJS

The United States does not seem interested in determining why it has the highest incarceration rate in the world and appears uninterested in reducing the rate. With White men in there 20's representing only 1.6 percent of prison inmates and Blacks representing 12 percent, there is not much chance that the government will work to reduce the number of Blacks in prison even though their percentage is well above the national average. **It is up to the Black population to reduce the Black prison population**.

Prisons represent a nation's failure. The more prisons a nation have the greater its failure.

Blacks are 47.7% of the Murder Victims

In 2008, 14,299 persons were murdered in the United States. Eighty percent were males. Blacks accounted for 6,826 of the total or 47.7% even though the Black population is around 12% of the nation. Included in the Black deaths were 1,019 Black teenagers ages 13 to 19. Between the ages 20 to 24, 1,435 Blacks were killed and from age 25 to 29, 1,224 Blacks were killed in 2008. These age groups represent the largest lost of life, see (Figure 13.5) below.

We are Losing the Future

There were more Black teenagers murdered in 2008 than 2001, see Figure 13.4 below.

Figure 13.4

Black Teenagers Murdered 2001 and 2008

Age	2001	2008
13 to 16 Yrs.	187	246
17 to 19 Yrs.	679	773
Total	866	1019

Source: U.S. Census Bureau 2011

Figure 13.5
Murder Victims by Race in 2008

Age	Total	White	Black	Other	Unknown
	14299	6907	6826	325	241
% Of Total	100	48.3	47.7	2.3	1.7
Infant to 12 Yrs.	712	406	257	30	21
13 to 16 Yrs.	448	193	246	7	2
17 to 19 Yrs.	1343	540	773	17	12
20 to 24 Yrs.	2457	962	1435	42	18
25 to 29 Yrs.	2163	868	1224	45	26
Total Under 29 Yrs.	7123	2969	3935	141	79
30 Yrs. & Older	7176	3938	2891	184	162

Source: U.S. Federal Bureau of Investigation
Found under: U.S. Census Bureau 2011 Table #307

Violent crime can be reduced by over 90% if the nation increased its level of education

Most violent crimes are committed by persons with 12 years or less of education.

The United States has not been willing to commit the resources needed to provide a quality education for all. The nation seems to be more interested in building prisons than building schools even though violent crime can be reduced by over 90% if the nation increased the level of education of its population. See (Figure 13.6) below showing the prisoner population under sentence of death in the year 2008 by education level. The higher the education levels the fewer violent crimes and the fewer number of prisoners under death.

Figure 13.6

Prisoners Under Sentence of Death in 2008

Years of School Completed	Number on Death Row	Percentage
7 years or less	176	6.6
8 years	185	6.9
9 to 11 years	977	36.8
12 years	1094	40.5
More than 12 years	247	9.2
Total	2679	100.0

Source: U.S. Census Bureau 2011

Other statistics from the Department of Justice:

The prevalence of imprisonment in 2001 was higher for
-- black males (16.6%) and Hispanic males (7.7%) than for white males (2.6%)
-- black females (1.7%) and Hispanic females (0.7%) than white females (0.3%)

Characteristics of State Prison inmates
Sixty-four percent of prison inmates belonged to racial or ethnic minorities in 2001.
An estimated 57% of inmates were under age 35 in 2001.
Altogether, an estimated 57% of inmates had a high school diploma or its equivalent.

Among the State prison inmates in 2000: -- nearly half were sentenced for a violent crime (49%) -- a fifth were sentenced for a property crime (20%) -- about a fifth were sentenced for a drug crime (21%)

Characteristics of jail inmates

Women were 10% of the local jail inmates in 1996, unchanged from 1989.
Forty-eight percent of jailed women reported having been physically or sexually abused prior to admission; 27% had been raped.
Sixty-three percent of jail inmates belonged to racial or ethnic minorities in 1996, up slightly from 61% in 1989.
Twenty-four percent of jail inmates were between the ages of 35 and 44 in 1996, up from 17% in 1989.
Over a third of all inmates reported some physical or mental disability.
Altogether, 54% of inmates had a high school diploma or its equivalent.
Thirty-six of all inmates were not employed during the month before they were arrested for their current offense -- 20% were looking for work; 16% were not looking.
Among the local jail inmates in 1996: -- a fourth were held for a violent crime -- a fourth were held for a property crime -- about a fifth were held for a drug crime
More than 7 of every 10 jail inmates had prior sentences to probation or incarceration.

A quarter of the jail inmates said they had been treated at some time for a mental or emotional problem.

Cost of Corrections

In 2006 $68,747,203,000 was spent on corrections. Average State cost per inmate $22,650 per year.

Power to the People

The criminal system in the United States is built to capture, prosecute, and jail Blacks. The high number of Blacks being sent to prison comes from the following:

    A) Blacks breaking the law.
    B) Blacks accused of breaking the law but do not have the money to hire good legal representation.
    C) Blacks being profiled by the police.
    D) Blacks being tried by prejudice juries.

    A) The best way to Handle Blacks breaking the Law is for Blacks not to break the law.

    1) Don't use or sell illegal drugs. Will lead to jail.
    2) Don't force anyone to do anything they do not want to do. Can lead to a fight and jail.
    3) Don't fight girl friends, spouses, office workers, relatives, neighbors or anyone else. Can lead to jail and arrest record.
    4) Don't forge checks or any other type of documents. Can lead to jail and arrest record.
    5) Don't drink. Can lead to spousal and child abuse and arrest.
    6) Don't drink and drive. Can lead to drunken driver arrest.
    7) Don't drive without a good driver's license. Can lead to arrest.
    8) Follow the rules of the road when driving, i.e. don't speed, obey stop signs, and know your State's driving laws. You can save money and stay out of jail.
    9) Pay your bills on time. You can avoid being sued and imprisoned and at the same time maintain good credit.
    10) Don't get mad at anyone. Anger can cause you to do something you would not normally do. Negotiate differences.
    11) Don't steal, rob or kill.

    In other words, just obey the law.

B) <u>The Best way to have good Legal Representation is to be Prepared</u>

Put yourself in a position where you have enough money to defend yourselves and your family. The judicial system in the United States is not always fair to Blacks and you must be prepared to defend yourself against it. Establish a legal fund. Join a company that has legal benefits. Develop or join a legal group. Know the law. If it is a false arrest, sue the police department because if the police department does not pay for its mistakes it is bound to repeat them.

C) <u>The best way to beat Police Profiling is to Hold Elected Official Accountable</u>

Join community groups and fight police profiling. Require reports on who is stopped, where, and for what reason.
Hold the individual police officer and the police department accountable for their actions. Set up a community review board. Elect people to office that will end police profiling. Make the police work for you and not against you.

D) <u>The best way to beat Unfair Juries is to organize</u>

Develop data banks of where police, juries and courts practice racism. Identify their locations in the country and isolate these problem areas. If the individual or area cannot be rehabilitated develop ways to minimize their impact on Blacks and society.

These areas can be identified just like some travel companies identify speed traps. An example is Cicero, Illinois. Cicero was a very prejudiced town. Martin Luther King went to Cicero and tried to integrate the town. An angry White mob attacked King and drove him out. This town may be beyond rehabilitation and should be identified as such. Another example is Simi Valley, California. Based on the justice Rodney King received in their court system, you do not want to be stopped by the police or tried by one of their juries. Even with overwhelming evidence, the Simi Valley court system could not find justice.

Prejudice zones like these can be identified and listed in the data bank. From the data bank, Black motorist and travelers can be alerted to risk areas like Cicero and Simi Valley so that they can be avoided.

Benefits of a Declining Prison Population

Follow the law and in most cases, you can prevent being arrested thus keeping a clean record for when you are applying for a job, school grant, home mortgage or any of the other goals you are trying to reach.

It is up to the people who do not have good schools to build them and it is also up to the people who do not have jobs to create them. Blacks cannot wait for Whites to build the Black community. Blacks must build schools to achieve quality education and build businesses to create jobs. When this is accomplished, the Black prison population will decline.

Summary of Chapter 13 – Crime

The message is simple here. Blacks need to obey the laws thus reducing the number of Blacks with criminal records thus increasing the number of Blacks with jobs.

1) Crime is destroying the Black Community with nearly 900,000 Black men in jail.
2) Because of criminal record, Blacks are excluded from thousands of jobs.
3) In 2006, an estimated 12 percent of all black men in their 20's were in jail or prison.
4) The United States is doing little to eliminate the root causes of crime.

5) Blacks accounted for 48% of the murder victims in the United States even though the Black population is around 12% of the nation.

6) Violent crime (prisoners under sentence of death) can be reduced by nearly 90% if the nation increased its education level to more than 12 years.

7) Blacks obeying the laws and establishing defense against those who would falsely accuse Blacks of crimes can reduce the number of Blacks in prison. Defense includes suing for false arrest, electing officials that end police profiling and identifying prejudice zones.

8) It is up to Blacks to reduce crime by building schools and providing a quality education and building businesses to provide a job where the education can be used.

Chapter 14 – Drinking:

If the Black community took all the money it spends on alcohol and invested it in appreciating assets there would not be enough poverty in the Black community to fill a shot glass.

The Black community drinks far too much alcohol and has far too little determination to stop. A percentage of 60.2 of Black males drink and 47.7 percentage of Black females drink in 2009, an increase over 2000, see (Figure 14.1 and 14.2) on consumption below. Black females had a larger increase than Black men.

Although the percentage of Blacks who drink is less than the other races, because of the high rate of poverty in the Black community, any drinking poses a barrier to Black prosperity.
The National Institute on Drug Abuse (NIDA) estimates that alcohol abuse cost the Black community $20,300,000,000 billion dollars per year. This money could be used to build the Black community, not destroy the Black community.

Figure 14.1

Alcohol Consumption 18 Years and Older-Percentage of Current Drinkers among all Persons

	Male	Male	Male	Female	Female	Female
Race	1997	2000	2009	1997	2000	2009
White	71.8	69.7	74.0	60.7	59.9	63.2
Black	56.9	56.2	60.2	40.9	39.4	47.7
Hispanic	64.6	63.7	65.7	42.1	41.2	43.8
American Indian or Alaskan Native	66.1	62.6	64.9	45.2	46.9	49.0
Asian	60.1	55.9	58.2	31.6	29.3	34.6

Source: NCHS

Figure 14.2

Alcohol Consumption 18 Years and Older-Percentage of Persons with 5 or more drinks on at least one day

Race	Male 1997	Male 2000	Male 2009	Female 1997	Female 2000	Female 2009
White	32.8	29.9	35.9	13.5	12.1	16.5
Black	18.4	19.8	21.5	6.5	5.2	8.4
Hispanic	30.9	27.9	30.4	9.7	6.8	9.2
American Indian or Alaskan Native	45.7	29.2	33.5	18.1	19.0	14.9
Asian	17.8	14.1	16.7	5.2	3.7	5.4

Source: NCHS Table 65.

Advertising Booze to the Black Community

The advertising industry has built phony icons in the Black community that pretends to represent a right of passage for young Black males and to some extent Black females. That symbol is that to come of age you need to drink. I once watched a 16-year-old girl drink a whole bottle of scotch. There was a ribbon on the bottle, which she removed, and placed around her neck and proudly declared her womanhood for consuming the entire bottle. Later that night, I heard that she had to be rushed to the hospital because of the high content of alcohol in her body and she just nearly escaped death.

Alcohol has been the curse of the Black and the poor communities for decades. The alcohol industry has targeted the less informed segment of the population to peddle their hazardous products and it has had a devastating effect on the Black community.

The role of Alcohol in Crime Victimization

The Bureau of Justice Statistics/Criminal Victimization offers the following information:

About 1 million violent crimes occur in which victims perceived the offender to have been drinking at the time of the offense.

Two-thirds of the victims who suffered violence by an intimate (a current or former spouse, boyfriend, or girlfriend) reported that alcohol had been a factor. Among spouse victims, 3 out of 4 incidents were reported to have involved an offender who had been drinking.

Use of Alcohol by Convicted Offenders

Per the Bureau of Justice Statistics/Criminal Victimization,
among the 5.3 million convicted offenders under the jurisdiction of corrections agencies, nearly 2 million, or about 38%, were estimated to have been drinking at the time of the offense.

Alcohol use at the time of the offense was commonly found among those convicted of public-order crimes which is a type of offense most highly represented among those on probation and in jail. Among violent offenders, 41% of those in local jails, 38% of those in State prisons, and 20% of those in Federal prisons were estimated to have been drinking when they committed the crime.

Intimate Victimizers

Per the Bureau of Justice Statistics/Criminal Victimization,
about 4 in 10 inmates serving time in jail for intimate violence had a criminal justice status of on probation or parole, or under a restraining order at the time of the violent attack on an intimate.
About 1 in 4 convicted violent offenders confined in local jails had committed their crime against an intimate; about 7% of State prisoners serving time for violence had an intimate victim.

About half of all offenders convicted of intimate violence and confined in a local jail or a State prison had been drinking at the time of the offense. Jail inmates who had been drinking prior to the intimate violence consumed an average amount of ethanol equivalent to 10 beers.

About 8 in 10 inmates serving time in State prison for intimate violence had injured or killed their victim.

Alcohol can bring poverty, fear and death to the family

Even though the death or injury of a person involved in an alcohol related event is enough, this is only the beginning of the tragedy. Families without fathers, children without dads, mothers without spouses, have all contributed to the decline of the foundation of the Black family. The family support system is gone in many cases and it has been replaced by poverty and crime which leads to more of the same in an out of control society break down. As more crimes lead to more jails, Blacks are pulled farther and farther into poverty. Fueled by alcohol, desperation and despair has engulfed almost a fourth of the Black community.

Drunks are a Danger to the Black Family

Drunken fathers, husbands and boyfriends are a real and present danger in the Black community. I can recall, a son shooting his father because the father in a drunken rage was beating up the mother. I know families who fear the return of their spouse or father after he has been out drinking. The image of a playful drunk is not the reality these families face. Their reality is far more menacing and dangerous and could and has lead to their injury and death.

Danger Cloaked in Fancy Wrapping

The sellers of alcohol will not warn you of the dangers their product's represents. In fact, they will present their products in fancy wrappings. Take for example the booze industry. Their bottles are designed to convey a sense of power or wealth and not the alcohol dependency that the product actually delivers. Often their commercials present actors dressed in tuxedoes, attending up scale parties in grand ballrooms drinking expensive liquor. These ads do not show the alcohol-addicted housewife in her bathrobe at 8am in the morning clutching her second drink even before the sun has risen. Nor do their ads show the normally reliable husband or father assaulting and brutalizing his wife and children after he has had too much to drink.

Benefits of not drinking to the Black Community

Alcohol abuse is costing the Black community $20,300,000,000 billion a year.

Eliminating the consumption of alcohol in the Black community can be one of the most profound and beneficial achievements in the history of the Black race.

By eliminating alcohol, spousal and child abuse related to drinking would end. The fear and physical danger from a drunken father or spouse would be replaced with respect and support. The family would be safer and stronger to pursue the higher goals in life like a college education or a business venture or simply helping others in the community.

The elimination of alcohol would also enhance the standard of living in the Black community. People would go to work not under the influence of alcohol. Productivity would increase which could bring an increase in income. Also, income that was spent on booze could go to investments, education and ventures that add to your wealth instead of subtracting from your wealth.

One of the most profound changes that can be achieved by eliminating alcohol from the Black community is the social advancement of the race. Fighting due to alcohol would end which means no more domestic quarrels. No alcohol related fighting in the streets, bars, parks or concerts. This also means that there would be no one arrested for disturbing the peace. No arrest records to harm credit reports or negatively impact a potential employer's inquiry.

Eliminating alcohol would reduce cost in the community. Drinking cost money, 20.3 billion dollars per years in the Black community. This includes not only the cost of the product but also the cost related to the product. The cost includes, the cost of losing your family due to a drinking problem, cost of being arrested for driving drunk, cost of injuring or killing someone in a car accident, cost of rehabilitation from alcohol, cost of losing a job due to alcohol, cost of not being able to get a job due to a drinking problem, and the cost of medical treatment for liver disease and other related illness.

Where to Find Help to Stop Drinking

1. Alcohol and Drug Abuse Hotline   800-521-7128

2. National Council on Alcoholism and
   Drug Dependence.   800-622-2255
   www.ncadd.orgn

3. National Clearinghouse for Alcohol
   and Drug Information.   800-676-1730
   HigherEDCtr@edc.org

4. Center for Substance Abuse   877-726-4727
   Treatment
   www.samhsa.gov

5. Alcoholics Anonymous (AA)
   www.alcoholics-anonymous.org
   or see local telephone directories for phone number.

Chapter Fourteen – Drinking Summary:

1) A total of 60.2 percent of the Black male population drank in 2009. Also, 47.7 percent of the Black female population drank in 2009.
2) The alcohol industry targets Blacks.
3) Alcohol contributes to the high crime rate in the Black community.

4) Alcohol brings poverty, fear, and death to the Black family.
5) The elimination of drinking in the Black community will bring great benefits.
6) Alcohol hotlines are available to help people to stop drinking.

Chapter 15 – Drugs

Using Illegal drugs is costing the Black community $13,400,000,000 billion per year.

We are doing it to ourselves; therefore our destiny is in our hands.

No one is forcing Blacks to take drugs. No one is sticking needles in their arms or forcing drugs up their nose. Taking drugs is a personal choice. A choice we can change by deciding that our lives will be a lot more fulfilling and productive if we do not use illegal drugs. Blacks should make a commitment that they will not use illegal drugs.

The benefits of not using illegal drugs to the Black community are vast. Listed below are some.

1) Money spent on drugs can go to obtaining a college degree or starting a business.
2) Without drugs in the body, a person will be able to think and function better on the job or at their business.
3) Blacks being arrested for illegal drugs would disappear. No more drug arrest records. No more posting bail for arrest. No more costly lawyers to defend arrested drug users.
4) The portion of the Black prison population related to drugs would vanish.
5) Since drugs are present when most crimes are committed in the community we can reduce violent crimes, property loss, domestic violence and driving while intoxicated by eliminating the use of drugs.
6) Decreasing the demand for illegal drugs would go a long way toward ending drug purchases.

African Americans make up 12.2 % of the US population but 59% of those convicted of drug offenses.

Illegal Drugs will cost you Time and Money

Illegal drugs should be avoided at all cost. Not only will they control your life but they will also destroy your life.

The Drug Policy Alliance states that, although African Americans make up 12.2 % of the US population and 13% of the drug users, they are 38% of those arrested for illegal drugs and 59% of those convicted of drug offenses. Some would even say that the war on drugs is the "New Jim Crow".

The New Jim Crow

Lets just say that the war on drugs is the "New Jim Crow", if so then this is a war Blacks can win by simply not using illegal drugs. This is an easy win without having to spend a dime. In fact by not purchasing illegal drugs you save money. It is also a must win because the use of illegal drugs is having a devastating effect on the Black community. It has resulted in the lost of jobs, parents not taking care of their children, students dropping out of school, financial obligations not being met, families breaking up, spouses and children being abused and the expenditure of large sums of money to defend persons accused of using and selling drugs. This is a huge waste of money and lives and a cost the Black community cannot afford.

Drug Use Contributes to the High Black Mortality Rate

One of the top reasons why so many Blacks are in prison is because they were arrested for possession of illegal drugs. Having a record for illegal possession of drugs is one of the first steps down a slippery slope to poor health and a shortened life cycle. With a drug addiction, many young Blacks never finish high school. Not completing high school usually means that you will not go to college or technical school. Without a college degree or technical training, a person's chance of getting a good job is usually poor. Without a good job, a person will probably not have health insurance. Without health insurance, medical problems will probably not be addressed and over the years will worsen which could lead to an early death. Lack of medical care and poor diets have lead to the high Black mortality rate, see Figure 15.1.

Figure 15.1

Life Expectancy Year 2000 and 2007

Race/ethnicity	Year 2000	Year 2007
All Races:	76.8	77.9
Male	74.1	75.4
Female	79.3	80.4
White Both Sex:	77.3	78.4
White Male	74.7	75.9
White Female	79.9	80.8
Black Both Sexes:	71.8	73.6
Black Male	68.2	70.0
Black Female	75.1	76.8

Source: CDC

Arrestee Drug Abuse Monitoring Program

The tables below are provided to give the scope of the drug problems and some of its consequences.

The tables are from the Arrestee Drug Abuse Monitoring Program – ADAM II 2008 Adult Male Program Finding, Part of the Department of Justice. Also, similar information is provided on female drug use for 2002.

Four representative cities are listed, Atlanta, Chicago, New York, and Washington D.C. These cities have large Black populations and frequent drug arrest. There are some recurring patterns in all of these cities.

Arrest Rate of Black Men can be 8 Times Greater

The arrest of Black men is eight times the arrest record of White men; see Washington D.C. (Figure 15.2) below. Also Black females are not spared this anomaly. In Cleveland, Ohio, a Black woman is almost three times more likely to be arrested than a White female, see (Figure 15.5) on females arrested below.

Figure 15.2

Summary of Adult Males Arrested by Percentage and Race in Atlanta, Chicago, New York and Washington for 2008

City	Black	White	Hispanic	Other
Atlanta	77.4	12.2	10.5	0.8
Chicago	64.7	10.6	23.0	1.2
New York	37.1	13.0	45.8	3.7
Washington D.C.	85.3	1.0	7.7	5.3

Source: ADAM II – Year 2008
Data will not add to 100% because arrestees may identify as multiple races.

Crime can be reduced by 95% by Increasing Education

The national crime rate could be reduced by 95% by increasing the education level of the nation to a four-year college degree or greater.

The greater the level of education, the fewer arrested. The Figure 15.3 below shows that the higher a persons level of education the less likelihood that a person will be arrested for violent crimes, property theft, drug abuse, domestic violence and driving while intoxicated. Persons without high school diploma or a GED, make up 41.0 percent of the arrestees. Persons with a four-year college degree or higher, make up 4.9 percent of the arrestees. The table suggests that if everyone in the nation had a college degree, the national crime rate would be reduced by 95%. Vocational and Trade School persons also have a low arrest record.

Figure 15.3

Highest Educational Level of Arrestees by City (%)

Education Level	Percentage of Arrestees
None	31.2
High School or GED	41.0
Vocational or Trade School	3.4
Some college or two year associate	19.5
Four year degree or higher	4.9

Source: Arrestee Drug Abuse Monitoring Program – ADAM II – Annual Report 2008

Drugs Play a Major Role in Crime

Marijuana is not as innocent a drug as some would make it out to be. The ADAM study shows that it is present in 50.1% of violent offenses in Chicago, see summary (Figure 15.4) below. Also, this table points out that drugs showed up in 91.3% of the property offenses in Chicago. In New York drugs were present in 58.5% of the persons arrested for violent offenses.

Figure 15.4

Percentage Of Male Positive for Drugs by Offense – Atlanta, Chicago, New York, Washington DC

Cities/Crimes	Violent	Property	Drugs Possession	Drug Distribution
Atlanta:				
Any Drugs	55.4	78.7	87.6	N/A
Cocaine	21.0	58.5	39.1	N/A
Marijuana	37.3	37.5	64.5	N/A
Chicago:				
Any Drugs	67.9	91.3	91.2	65.1
Cocaine	10.2	56.7	54.5	24.3
Marijuana	50.1	41.3	55.3	37.7
New York:				
Any Drugs	58.5	68.2	95.6	80.2
Cocaine	19.2	34.0	35.6	33.9
Marijuana	42.7	40.9	67.2	69.5
Washington DC:				
Any Drugs	19.8	62.5	N/A	100.0
Cocaine	N/A	60.3	31.7	N/A
Marijuana	24.7	52.5	33.9	N/A

Source: Arrestee Drug Abuse Monitoring Program – ADAM II – Annual Report 2008

Police Action plays a minimum role in Reducing Drug Sale

Police action does not seem to play a major role in preventing the sell or use of drugs, see (Figure 15.5) below which shows failed drug buy due to police action. Atlanta GA has one of the lowest rates for police action to prevent drug sale.

The chart shows that police action accounted for 2.9% of the reasons a drug purchase was not made. Most drug users say that unavailability of drugs is the major reason way they were unable to buy drug. It could be argued that other earlier police action, like sea and border interdiction is the reason that a dealer did not have the quality or quantity of drugs desired but from this chart; it appears that police action will not solve the drug problem. It appears that decreasing the demand for illegal drugs would go a long way toward ending drug purchases.

Figure 15.5

Percentage of Failed Drug Buy Due to Police Activity in Past 30 Days 2007 and 2008

Drug	Marijuana	Marijuana	Crack Cocaine	Crack Cocaine
Year	2007	2008	2007	2008
Atlanta	25.5	13.9	7.2	2.9
Chicago	15.4	15.3	11.1	11.8
New York	14.8	7.7	14.7	16.8

Source: ADAM II – Year 2008

Black Females are a high percentage of Female Arrestees

Cleveland and Washington D.C. was selected to represent the Black female population because they both have a large number of Black females and arrestees.
Black females like Black males are more likely to be arrested than White females see (Figure 15.6). As with other groups, the higher the education level, the lower the number of Black females arrested, see (Figure 15.7) below.

Figure 15.6

Summary of Adult Females Arrested by Percentage and Race in Cleveland and Washington for 2002

City	Black	White	Hispanic	Other	Unknown
Cleveland	70.1	28.0	1.5	0	0.3
Washington D.C.	87.2	11.5	0	0	1.3

Source: ADAM – Year 2002

Figure 15.7

Highest Educational Level of Female Arrestees in Cleveland and Washington D.C (%)

Education Level	Cleveland	Washington D.C.
None	38.7	24.1
High School or GED	28.4	48.1
Vocational or Trade School	4.5	1.9
Some college or two year associate	26.2	16.7
Four year degree or higher	2.2	9.3

Source: ADAM – Year 2002

Figures (15.8, 15.9, 15.10, 15.11) below show the type and amount of drugs present in female arrestees.

Figure 15.8
Percentage of Female Arrestees using Drugs in Cleveland by Race and Type of Drug for 2002

Cleveland			
Race	Black	White	Hispanic
Any Drugs	64.4	64.3	50.0
Cocaine	44.4	38.1	25.0
Marijuana	27.2	23.8	25.0
Heroin	5.2	9.5	0
Methamphetamine	0.4	2.4	0
PCP	6.0	6.0	0
Multiple Drug	17.2	13.1	0

Source: ADAM – Year 2002

Figure 15.9

Percentage Of Female Positive for Drugs by Offense in Cleveland for 2002

Cleveland					
Crimes	Violent	Property	Drugs	Domestic Violence	Driving Intoxicated
Any Drugs	54.5	58.6	82.0	57.1	50.0
Cocaine	20.0	33.3	66.7	42.9	0
Marijuana	36.2	33.3	25.2	21.4	50.0
Heroin	5.5	3.4	7.2	0	0
Methamphetamine	0	3.4	0.9	0	0
PCP	3.6	6.9	7.2	0	0
Multiple Drug	12.7	17.2	22.5	7.1	0

Source: ADAM – Year 2002

Figure 15.10

Percentage of Female Arrestees using Drugs in Washington D.C. by Race and Type of Drug for 2002

Washington D.C.			
Race	Black	White	Hispanic
Any Drugs	69.4	100.0	0
Cocaine	36.1	50.0	0
Marijuana	30.6	50.0	0
Heroin	13.9	50.0	0
Methamphetamine	0	0	0
PCP	11.1	0	0
Multiple Drug	22.2	50.0	0

Source: ADAM – Year 2002

Figure 15.11

Percentage Of Female Positive for Drugs by Offense in Washington D.C. for 2002

Washington D.C.			
Crimes	Violent	Property	Drugs
Any Drugs	46.2	100.0	100.0
Cocaine	7.7	66.7	55.6
Marijuana	23.1	33.3	44.4
Heroin	7.7	33.3	44.4
Methamphetamine	0	0	0
PCP	23.1	16.7	0
Multiple Drug	15.4	50.0	44.4

Source: ADAM – Year 2002

Drug Dependence

Using drugs is one of the easiest trips to dependence. Over a third of the males who start to take drugs end up as dependent to the drug, see Male Risk of Dependency & Abuse for Washington, D.C. (Figure 15.12) below. The Department of Justice states that 32% of the Black male population has criminal records. Using Washington D.C. as a sample of the rest of the nation and multiplying the risk of dependency 34% by the approximately 5,440,000 Black males with criminal records (17,000,000 million Black males in the United States X 32% criminal rate = 5,400,000), a total of 1,836,000 (5,400,000 X 34% dependency rate) Black men have the potential of being a drug addict. Also, a total of 1,026,000 million Black men could become dependent on alcohol (rate of dependency for alcohol 19% X 5,400,000 million Black men).

The dependency for females could be even worse. Females have a dependency rate of 48% for drugs and 26% for alcohol see (Figure 15.13) for females in Cleveland.

Figure 15.12

Male Risk of Dependency & Abuse for Washington, D.C

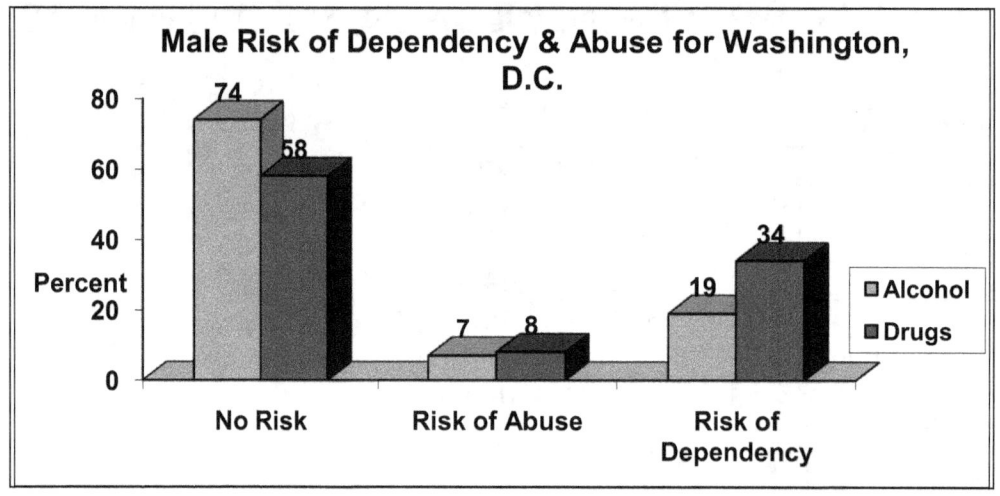

Source: Arrestee Drug Abuse Monitoring Program - ADAM
2002 Adult Male Program Finding

Figure 15.13

Female Risk of Dependency & Abuse for Cleveland, Ohio

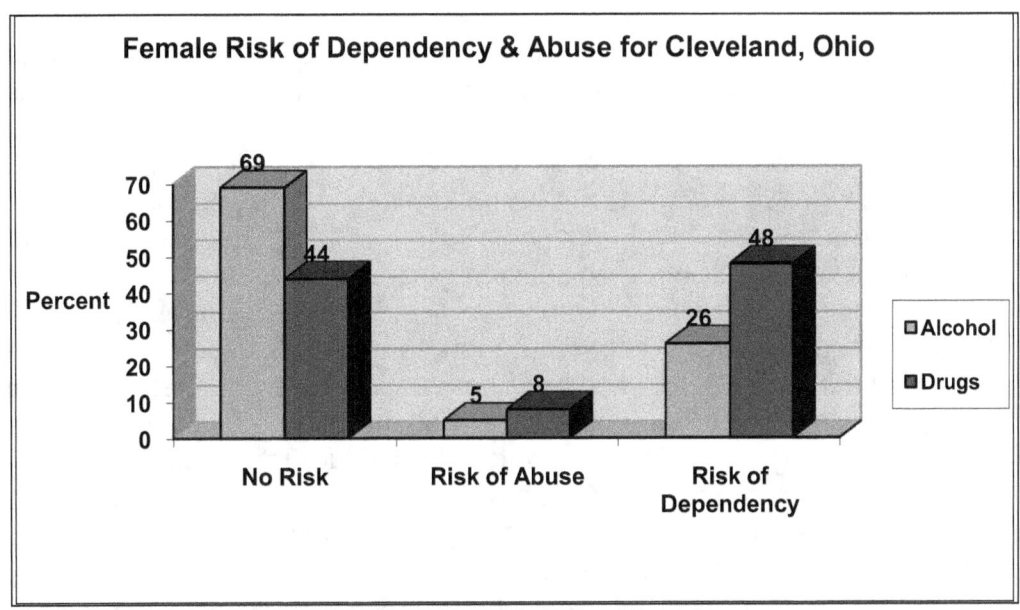

Arrestee Drug Abuse Monitoring Program - ADAM
2002 Adult Female Program Finding

Be aware that even legal drugs can be addictive and their use should be on a must use basis.

Drug Treatment

The best drug treatment is not to use drugs in the first place.

The organization <u>Drugnet</u> – The Drug & Alcohol Treatment & Prevention Global Network (www.drugnet.net) provides the following information on drug treatment.

- What are the four most common types of treatment? The four most common types of programs are outpatient methadone, outpatient drug-free, long-term residential, and short-term inpatient. Outpatient methadone programs administer the medication methadone to reduce cravings for heroin and block its effects. Counseling, vocational skills development, case management, and access support services are used to gradually stabilize the patient's functioning. Some patients stay on methadone for long periods, while others move from methadone to abstinence. Long-term residential programs offer around-the-clock, drug-free treatment in a residential community of counselors and fellow recovering addicts. Patients generally stay in these programs several months or up to a year or more. Some of these programs are referred to as therapeutic communities. Outpatient drug-free programs use a wide range of approaches including problem-solving groups, specialized therapies such as insight-oriented psychotherapy, cognitive-behavioral therapy, and 12-step programs. As with long-term residential treatment programs, patients may stay in these programs for months or longer. Short-term inpatient programs keep patients up to 30 days. Most of these programs focus on medical stabilization, abstinence, and lifestyle changes. Staff members are primarily medical professionals and trained counselors. Once primarily for alcohol abuse treatment, these programs expanded into drug abuse treatment in the 1980s.

- Is treatment effective? The four most common forms of drug abuse treatment are all effective in reducing drug use. That is the major finding from a NIDA-sponsored nationwide study of drug abuse treatment outcomes. The Drug Abuse Treatment Outcome Study (DATOS) tracked

10,010 drug abusers in nearly 100 treatment programs in 11 cities who entered treatment between 1991 and 1993.

- What makes patients stay in treatment? DATOS researchers found that the major predictors were high motivation, legal pressure to stay in treatment, no prior trouble with the law, getting psychological counseling while in treatment, and lack of other psychological problems, especially antisocial personality disorder. The investigators found that programs with low retention rates tended to have patients with the most problems, particularly antisocial personality disorder, cocaine addiction, or alcohol dependence.

- Do short term inpatient programs work? Short-term inpatient treatment programs in the DATOS study yielded significant declines in drug use, even though patients stayed in these programs no more than 30 days.

Drug Treatment Organizations:

Listed below are organizations that treat drug addiction. There are many more and a person should investigate and determine what is the best method for them to escape drugs.

1. National Alcoholism and Substance Abuse 800-252-6465
2. Cocaine Anonymous   800-347-8998
3. Marijuana Anonymous   800-766-6779
4. National Council on Alcoholism and
    Drug Dependence   800-676-1730
5. National Clearinghouse for Alcohol
    & Drug Information   800-729-6686
6. Center for Substance Abuse Treatment   877-726-4727

Drugnet, also list three organizations as their top choice for finding information on the Internet for drug abuse treatment:

1) The National Institute on Drug Abuse (NIDA), Information@ lists.nida.nih.gov or call 301-443-1124

This site can be used to begin a search for information and online resources for drug abuse treatment. Their mission is to provide strategic support and conduct of research across a broad range of disciplines and is aimed at improving addiction prevention, treatment, and policy.

2) The Center for Substance Abuse Treatment (CSAT) (http://csat.samhsa.gov)

CSAT works cooperatively across the private and public treatment spectrum to identify, develop, and support policies, approaches, and programs that enhance and expand treatment services for individuals who abuse alcohol and other drugs and that address individuals' addiction-related problems.

3) Join Together (www.jointtogether.org)

Join Together is a national resource center for communities working to reduce substance abuse and gun violence. Join Together has a vast library of resources and information on drug abuse treatment and advocacy, and is a must see site for anybody involved in the addiction field.

Other important organizations include: The National Institute on Alcoholism and Alcohol Abuse (NIAAA), Alcoholics Anonymous and Narcotics Anonymous.

Summary of Chapter 15 – Drugs

1) Using Illegal drugs is costing the Black community $13,400,000,000 billion per year.
2) African Americans make up 12.2% of the US population but 59% of those convicted of drug offenses.
3) Use of illegal drugs is having a devastating effect on the Black community.
4) Drug Use contributes to the high Black mortality rate.
5) Arrest rate for Black men can be eight times the rate for White men.

6) The nation's crime rate can be reduced 95% by increasing the level of education.
7) Marijuana and other drugs play a major role in crime.
8) Police action plays a minimum role in reducing drug sell.
9) Black females are high percentages of arrestees.
10) Drug dependency for Black females is 48%. For Black males it is 34%.
11) The four most common types of drug treatment programs are outpatient methadone, outpatient drug-free, long-term residential and short-term inpatient.
12) The most effective drug treatment program is not to start taking drugs in the first place.
13) Drug treatment organizations are available. See list above or go to the Internet.

Chapter 16 – Smoking:

An estimated 45,000 African Americans die from smoking-related diseases yearly.

Smoking Kills over 440,000 Americans a Year

Smoking is an industry with a past and a present that is nothing short of criminal. Smoking products kill over 440,000 people in the United States and millions of people through out the world yearly. It kills more people than all the world wars and it can do it legally and at a profit. Smoking is so addictive, that even those who are aware of its health hazards continue to smoke until they smoke themselves to death. If there has ever been a product that should be taken from the market, tobacco is that product.

Cigarettes contain at least 69 distinct cancer-causing chemicals

Congress has failed to Protect Americans from Tobacco

Why has tobacco products not been declared illegal, in one word, profits. The tobacco companies make so much money from the millions of addictive customers that they can buy and sell nearly every government body that is suppose to regulate them. The tobacco company's law departments are well staffed and highly paid. Their lobbying group could probably convince the U.S Congress to return the Louisiana Purchase to France if the tobacco industry believed it would serve big tobaccos interest. Those in Congress who refuse to ban smoking should be forced from office. It is down to a healthy environment or an unhealthy smoked filled room.

National Smoking Ban

Tobacco products are so addictive that the best way to beat them is to never start to smoke in the first place. That way you will not have to spend the rest of your life trying to overcome a smoking addiction. Also, in order to try and save the smokers who are addicted and to save yourself from second hand smoke, a national law should be passed banning smoking. It will save millions of lives and billions of dollars.

Smoking can cause death to you and your family. Also, it can be a slow death, a process that drains your health and your wealth at the same time. **Smoking cost Blacks $19,000,000,000 billion a year**.

The American Lung Association provides the following information:

1) It is estimated that 45,000 Blacks die each year from smoking related illness.
2) A total of 5.7 million, 22.9% African American adults smoked cigarettes.
3) If current trends continue, about 500,000 African Americans now under the age of 18 will die of smoking-related diseases.
4) Tobacco companies have targeted both African Americans and Hispanics with intensive merchandising.
5) Cigarettes contain at least 69 distinct cancer-causing chemicals.
6) Smoking is directly responsible for 87 percent of lung cancer cases and causes most cases of emphysema and chronic bronchitis.
7) Smoking is a major factor in coronary heart disease and strokes.
8) Smoking in pregnancy accounts for an estimated 20 to 30 percent of low-birth weight babies, up to 14 percent of pre-term deliveries, and some 10 percent of all infant deaths.
9) Secondhand smoke involuntarily inhaled by nonsmokers from other people's cigarettes is responsible for approximately 3,000 lung cancer deaths annually in U.S. nonsmokers.

10) Current female smokers aged 35 years or older are 12 times more likely to die prematurely from lung cancer than nonsmoking females.

11) More American women die annually from lung cancer than any other type of cancer; for example, lung cancer will cause an estimated

65,700 female deaths in 2002, compared with 39,600 estimated female deaths caused by breast cancer.

12) Tobacco advertising encourages young people to begin a lifetime addiction of smoking before they realize the health dangers. Approximately 90 percent of smokers begin smoking before age 21.

Do not use tobacco products like cigarettes, cigars and chewing tobacco, which can cause lung and month cancer and spread other forms of cancer throughout the body.

The percentage of Blacks Who Smoke is Declining:

The percentage of Black males, who smoke, has declined from 33.9% in the 1990-1992 periods to 22.9% in 2009. Black female smokers declined from 23.1 to 18.8 for the same period see (Figure 16.1) below. The trend is in the right direction. The only thing that is missing is an accelerator. The sooner Blacks do not smoke the sooner their health will improve and their life expectancy will increase.

Figure 16.1

Percentage of Current Cigarette Smoking by Adults

	Male	Male	Male	Female	Female	Female
Year	1990-1992	1999-2000	2009	1990-1992	1999-2000	2009
All Races	27.9	25.1	23.1	23.7	21.2	18.1
White	27.4	25.2	25.0	24.3	22.2	20.7
Black	33.9	27.2	22.9	23.1	19.7	18.8
Hispanic	26.5	23.2	17.6	16.6	12.5	9.4
American Indian or Alaska Native	34.2	30.4	N/A	36.7	34.7	N/A
Asian	24.8	20.3	N/A	6.3	6.7	N/A

To find: NCHS/Fastats A to Z/under (S)/under Smoking Table 61
Source: CDC, NCHS, And National Health Interview Survey

More Education Less Smoking:

A person with a Bachelor's degree or higher is more likely not to smoke vs. a person without a college degree, see figures (Figure 16.2 - All Persons), (Figure 16.3 - Black Males) (Figure 16.4 - Black Females).

Figure 16.2

Percentage of Current Cigarette Smoking Person 25 Years of Age by Education – All Persons

All Persons						
Year	1995	1997	1998	1999	2000	2009
No high school diploma or GED	35.6	33.5	34.4	32.2	31.9	29.7
High school diploma or GED	29.1	29.9	28.9	28.0	29.2	29.7
Some college, no bachelor degree	22.6	23.7	23.5	23.3	21.7	21.9
Bachelor's degree or higher	13.6	11.4	10.9	11.1	10.9	9.0

To find: NCHS/Fastats
Source: CDC, NCHS, and National Health Interview Survey

Figure 16.3

Percentage of Current Cigarette Smoking Person 25 Years of Age by Education – Black Males

Black Males						
Year	1995	1997	1998	1999	2000	2001
No high school diploma or GED	41.9	44.6	42.9	43.8	38.3	37.9
High school diploma or GED	36.6	39.0	32.8	32.5	29.1	33.4
Some college, no bachelor degree	26.4	27.0	28.4	23.4	20.0	24.2
Bachelor's degree or higher	17.3	14.5	15.3	11.3	14.7	11.3

To find: NCHS/Fastats A to Z/under (S)/under Smoking Table 60
Source: CDC, NCHS, And National Health Interview Survey

Figure 16.4

Percentage of Current Cigarette Smoking Person 25 Years of Age by Education – Black Females

Black Females						
Year	1995	1997	1998	1999	2000	2001
No high school diploma or GED	32.3	27.1	32.8	30.1	31.2	26.3
High school diploma or GED	27.8	29.1	24.3	22.4	25.4	21.3
Some college, no bachelor degree	20.8	24.3	21.7	22.3	20.4	17.4
Bachelor's degree or higher	17.3	12.5	9.0	13.4	10.8	11.6

To find: NCHS/Fastats A to Z/under (S)/under Smoking Table 60
Source: CDC, NCHS, and National Health Interview Survey

Minimize your risk to Tobacco

The only good news about smoking related deaths is that most of them are preventable. By following the suggestions below you can minimize your exposure to tobacco products.

1) Do not start to smoke.
2) If you have started smoking, quit.
3) Avoid contact with people who do smoke.

4) Stay off public transportation like airplanes, buses, trains, and ships that permit smoking. Stay out of restaurants, hotels, sporting facilities, schools, businesses and government buildings that permit smoking. This would also include buildings that permit smoking in part of the building.

5) Do not marry a smoker. Your health and the health of your children would be put at risk.

6) Do not work for a company that allows smoking on the job. You could lose more of your health than you could gain in your wallet.

7) Help establish private and public funds to prevent the start of smoking and the recovery of current smokers.

8) Protect children from smoke. They are too young to protect themselves.

9) Go after the source of the problem. Sue the tobacco industry again.

10) Establish federal laws banning smoking in all public places and in private places where employees are present.

Treatment for smoking addiction:

1. The Smokers' Hotline   800-638-0668
2. American Lung Association   800-586-4872
   Web: http://www.lungusa.org

Summary of Chapter 16 – Smoking

1) Smoking kills millions each year.
2) Congress has failed to protect the public from tobacco.
3) Smoking should be banned.
4) Smoking is costing Blacks $19,000,000,000 billion per year.
5) The American Lung Association has a long list of diseases and health problems that tobacco causes. The list includes lung cancer, emphysema, chronic bronchitis, coronary heart disease, strokes and low-birth weight in babies.
6) The percentage of Blacks who smoke is declining.
7) The more educated you are the more likely you will not smoke.

8) You can reduce your exposure to smoke by staying away from smokers and places that permit smokers like restaurants, sporting events and hotels.
9) Go after the source of the problem. Sue the tobacco industry.

Establish federal laws banning smoking in all public places and in private places where employees are present.

Chapter 17 – Military

Maximize Military Service

The military has always been a place of last resort where persons without income have gone to get a meal and a roof over their head. Blacks need to be looking for more than that. Although the service is an organization where you can meet some fine people from all walks of life, travel and eat three square meals a day, because Blacks are so far behind economically, Blacks need to pursue those careers that can maximize their potential. If you are in the service maximize your stay by becoming an officer or use the GI Bill to pay for your college or trade school education.

Military and Justice

The military is also an organization, where justice may not exist; at least it did not appear to be a priority when I was in the service.

I witness this in early 1968 around the time that Martin Luther King was murdered. I was in the Army at Fort Knox at a hand-to-hand combat training exercise. A young White sergeant who had recently returned from a tour in Vietnam was giving instructions to a young Black recruit on how to handle a bayonet. The bayonet was covered when the sergeant instructed the recruit to try and stab him with the weapon. The recruit tried but was blocked by the sergeant and tossed aside. The recruit said let me try again. The sergeant feeling more confident, removed the bayonet cover and said go ahead. Well, the results were predictable. The contest between the young Black from the ghetto and the young White male, back from a jungle war, ended in tragedy. The recruit thrust forward at the sergeant. The sergeant first said, see you missed. The recruit said no, I did not. The sergeant then smiled and admitted that the recruit did not miss and wobbled off the training platform, across a small patch of grass and collapsed in front of our platoon and died.

The Black recruit was taken away and the last word I heard, he would be charged with murder and tried by a military court. How fair was this? The Black recruit was first drafted into the military against his will and then forced to engage in a training exercise. Then tragically, but successfully completed his hand-to-hand combat training only to be arrested and tried by the organization that put him in that no win situation in the first place. If he lost the exercise, he would be a failure. If he won the exercise, he would be charged with murder.

Military Prisons

The high percentage of Blacks in military jails is not much better than the high percentage of Blacks in the civilian prisons see (Figure 17.1 and Figure 17.2) on military jails below. They show that out of a total of 2,747 military prisoners, 974 are Black or 35%. The Army has the most number of Blacks in prison at 503 or 45% of their prison population. The total number of prisoners in military jails did decrease in 2007, see Figure 17.3.

Also, the service is an organization where you can get bad papers or dishonorable discharges, which can prevent you from getting a good job for the rest of your life.
I had a little experience with Army justice during my stay in the Army. In 1969, after 364 days of being rocketed, mortared and shot at, my tour of duty in Vietnam was coming to a close. On my last day in country, several others and I who were headed home were charged with not taken part in a drill. A drill we had been excluded from to pack our bags. The officer in charge threatened to send us to the LBJ or Long Binh Jail in South Vietnam, which could lead to a dishonorable discharge. Never mind the fact that we had fought for our nation for an entire year and frankly were lucky to still to be alive and the fact that the charges were false. Fortunately, there was a quick investigation and we were exonerated. The next day, the charges were dropped and we departed that god forsaking land, but after that incident, I often wonder whose side is the Army on? I do not think they are on the side of the common soldier.

Figure 17.1

Military Prison Population by Race December 31, 1996

Branch of Service	Total Prison Population	White	Black	|Hispanic	Asians/Pacific
Air Force	487	322	125	20	20
Army	1106	476	503	88	39
Marine Corps	685	371	206	71	38
Navy	455	257	138	36	23
Coast Guard	14	7	2	6	1
Total	2,747	1433	974	219	121

Source: U.S. Department of Justice.
    Bureau of Justice Statistics April, 1999

Figure 17.2

Prisons Under Military Jurisdiction December 31, 1996

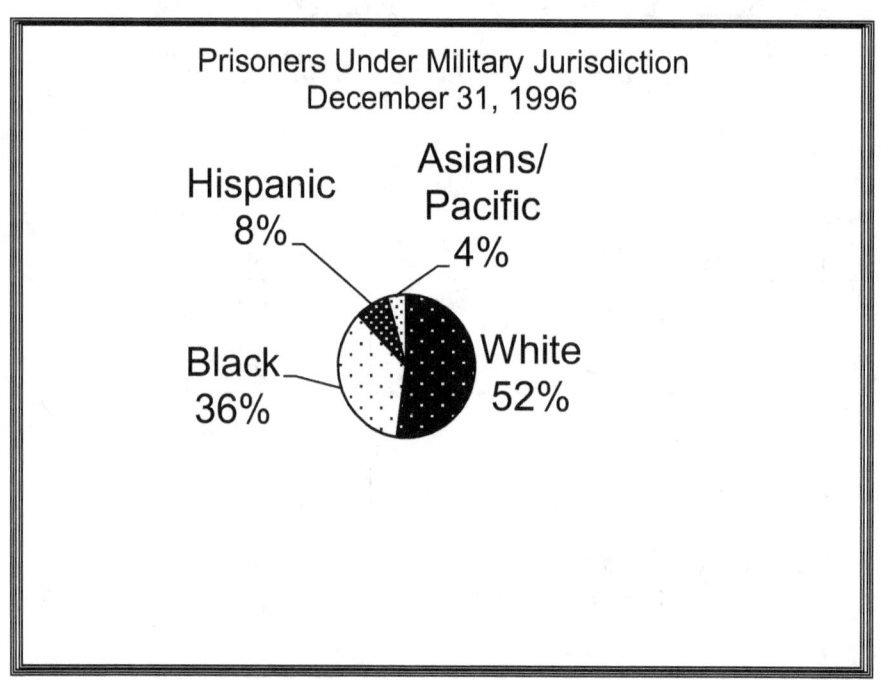

Prisoners Under Military Jurisdiction
December 31, 1996

Hispanic 8%

Asians/ Pacific 4%

Black 36%

White 52%

Source: U.S. Department of Justice - Bureau of Justice Statistics April 1999.

Figure 17.3

Military Prison Population for 2007

Branch of Service	Total Prison Population
Air Force	280
Army	829
Marine Corps	396
Navy	268
Coast Guard	21
Total	1794

Source: Bureau of Justice Statistics

The Military may not be the place to further your Education

The military may not be the place to receive or advance your education. In 1968, I graduated from college with a degree in Accounting. I was drafted into the military but was placed in a unit that had nothing to do with my education. I ended up in an artillery unit. My job was to plot targets and give range and directions to the guns. Now, we could put a round on top of a hut five miles away within seconds and blow away anything and everyone nearby, but where in corporate America is that skill needed? The military trains its personnel for military jobs. Don't expect the military to train you for civilian jobs. Civilian jobs are best learned in public and private schools 1-12, colleges, universities and trade schools.

Summary of Chapter 17 - Military

1) Maximize your stay in the military but remember the pay is lousy and the work is hazardous to your health.
2) Military justice may not exist.
3) Army military prisons are 45% Black
4) The military may not be a place to further your career.

Chapter 18 – Government

Everything you may have gained in life can be lost with one election.

Vote to Protect Your Family and Business

Participation in government is essential to protecting your family, business and your prosperity. Registering and voting is the corner stone to any economic success. Without a friendly government, freedom of movement can be lost, access to capital diminished, the right of ownership taken away and the protection of law and order denied.

Prior to the passing of the civil rights laws of the 1960's, the United States followed a policy of denying Black Americans the right to accumulate wealth. They carried out this policy with zeal and determination. Nearly every institution in the nation adhered to this policy including the banking system that refused commercial loans to the Black community, the real estate agencies that refused to sell homes to Blacks in so-called White neighborhoods, the legal system that did not protect Black's from police brutality, the business community that refused to hire Blacks in white collar jobs, and the education community, who restricted funding to Black schools and prevented Black students from going to so-called White schools. All of you have been a victim or have witnessed these atrocities in your lifetime. Who can forget the Alabama governor George Wallace standing in front of the public school door trying to prevent Black students from entering. Or can anyone forget the Los Angeles highway patrol clubbing and beating Black motorist Rodney King, or how often have major companies been sued over job discrimination or refusing service to Black people. Coca Cola and Denny's restaurant come to mind. Voting gives you the power to elect officials who can protect you against these crimes and at the same time give you the platform to accumulate wealth.

Vote to end Police Brutality

Black judges need to be elected to enforce the civil rights laws. Black mayors must also be elected to end police brutality and ensure that the police departments do not violate the rights of its citizens.
More Blacks need to be on juries. Often the juror is drawn from the registered vote list, so it is important to be registered.

Vote to Ensure Your Share of Government Contracts

Blacks need to be present when city contracts are proposed to ensure that city dollars are spread equally among the city's population. By electing Blacks to city offices, more Black firms will be at the table when the city contracts are awarded.

Vote for Governments that Support Black Business

The vote is needed to protect against government actions that may prevent a person from gaining wealth. An example could be a businessperson needing access roads to their plants. A city council that is supportive of your needs can provide the road permits and easements. In some cases, if you are bringing jobs to the community, the city government may even offer tax incentives and rebates. Or if land is needed, government through the use of eminent domain, can acquire property that would other wise not be available.
On the other hand, a city government that is hostile to your company can place barriers and road blocks in the way and drive the cost of doing business up so high that it would not be feasible to even start the project.

More Blacks need to Vote

Total voting in presidential elections has gone from 67.7 percent in 1992 to 63.6 percent in 2008 as shown in (Figure 18.1) below.

The percentage for Blacks voting in 1992 was 59.2%. In 2000, the percentage for Black voters went down to 56.8. In the 2008 election, probable due to the fact that an African American was running, 65.0 % of eligible Blacks voted.

The increased number of Black voters is good but the goal should be nothing less than 100% voter participation. Political power is needed to support and protect Black families and their businesses. See below the voting patterns of Blacks since 1992.

Figure 18.1

Voting in Presidential Elections

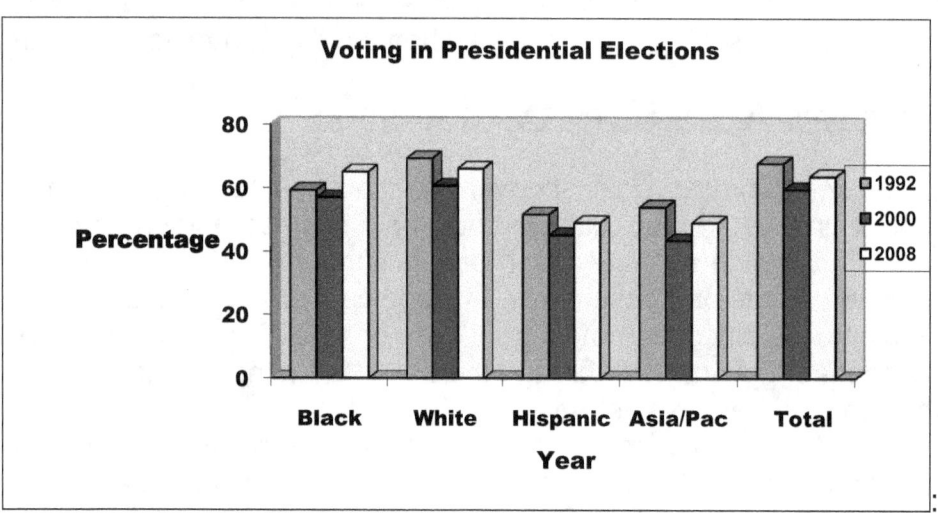

Source: US Census Bureau

Vote to Grow

Elect officials that will protect you from forces that attempt to prevent you from gaining education, acquiring businesses or accumulating wealth. Also, it is not enough to prevent others from attacking you, in order to move ahead, you must negate the attackers, and still acquire and employ the tools of wealth.

Summary of Chapter 18 - Government

1) Participation in government is essential to protecting your family, business and your prosperity.
2) Prevent police brutality by voting in the good people.
3) Gain your fair share of city contracts by voting into office those officials who will protect your business interest.
4) More Blacks need to Vote.
5) The percentage of Black voting should be 100%. Registering and voting is one of the cheapest and easiest ways to gain power and protect your economic base.

Conclusion

Black living conditions are intolerable

Living conditions for millions of Blacks in the United States have become intolerable. The poverty rate is over 25 percent. That means that for every fourth Black person you meet one will be living in poverty. Black unemployment over at least the last thirty years has been nearly twice the national average. Blacks are twelve percent of the general population but 39 percent of the prison population.

Blacks have one of the highest mortality rates in the nation.
Blacks score the lowest on national testing. Blacks make up less than one percent of the top corporate jobs. Blacks have one of the highest obesity rates in the nation at 78%. Blacks have the highest HIV death rate in the nation. Blacks have one of the highest percentages of unmarried mothers in the country. Black businesses represent only 2% of the Gross National Product.

Blacks must take charge

Affirmative action, government handouts and charity have failed to lift millions of Blacks out of poverty. It is clear that Blacks need a new approach to ending poverty and gaining prosperity. I believe that the new approach is for Blacks to take their destiny into their own hands. By controlling the process they can determine the outcome. The Black race must go from a poor, unorganized and undercapitalized community to a rich, well-managed and robust society. They must convert their institutions, customs and goals from begging to building, from consuming to providing, from depreciating assets to appreciating assets, from spending to saving, from jails to schools, from unhealthy to healthy, from law breaking to law making, from unwed mothers to two parent families, from gamblers to non gamblers, from drinkers to non drinkers, from drug users to non drug users, and from smokers to non smokers.

What an Adventure

Is there anything more exciting than the challenge that is before us? Is there anything more worthy of our energy and ability than to end poverty in our time? Funding will be needed to accomplish our goals. Blacks can build their corporations just like every other group in America by pooling resources, money and labor from individuals, intuitions and neighborhoods. Money should not be given it should be earned. Charity should be replaced by investments. Anyone funding the new corporations should expect a monetary return from their investment. Blacks need to go from welfare to nation building, from expecting a hand out to providing a hand up.

Resources

Many of the things Blacks can do to begin the process of ending poverty will not cost any money. In fact, many events will add money to the Black community, money that can be used to fund the business enterprises and community workshops in the Black community. For instance, currently Blacks are spending $53,000,000,000 billion a year on alcohol, drugs and smoking. Eliminating these vices will free up billions of dollars to fund the Black community. These funds could go into Black banks. The Black banks could then fund Black businesses. These businesses could then create jobs in the Black community. Vices, which today are destroying the Black community, could be turned around to build the Black community. Also, crime and the cost of crime could be eliminated making the Black community a safe and healthy place.

A Healthy Community

Just by eating healthier, the Black community will benefit. The cost of health care will actually go down. The mortality rate for Blacks will also go down, Blacks will live longer. Black parents will be around longer to help their offspring and grand children.

Education

It does not cost the Black community anything to speak English. Speaking English is the first step toward being able to write and read. Once you can speak, write and read English then you can master the other subjects like math and science. Once you know these subjects you are prepared for college. Once you graduate from college you are prepared to take on the world.

Cash Flow

Over $500,000,000,000 billion pass through Black hands each year. Blacks need businesses to capture and use this money to grow. Listed below are some suggestions on how to employ this money:
1) Put accountants in charge of your financial operations. They know how to penny pinch a dollar.
2) Put financiers and entrepreneurs in charge of business operations, they know how to expand a penny.
3) Save. End up with more each year.
4) Invest in safe and growing ventures.
5) Maximize every dollar, every income, and every business.

No Excuses

There are no excuses why Blacks should remain some of the poorest people in the world. We have the resources and the ability to prosper. We just need to say to ourselves that there are no excuses for failure and go out and build the community that is worthy of the Black race.

Appendix 1- Progress Chart

You can go from poverty to prosperity by completing the task below. The benefits are based on the amount of use. The more of the good things you do the greater the reward. Also, the less of the bad things you do the greater the reward. Follow this chart and you cannot lose.

Progress Chart Part I

Task	Date Accomplished	Benefits
Speak good English.		Learning starts with your ability to speak well.
Learn how to use the Internet.		Provides unlimited information and possibilities.
Develop good study habits.		As technology advances more studying will be required.
Take college prep courses in high school.		You will be better prepared for college.
Complete high school.		You will need a high school degree to get into college. Don't depend on GED to get by.
Complete college or trade school.		College provides the academics and the social exposure.

Progress Chart Part II

Task	Date Accomplished	Benefits
Get a job		Money, status and self-esteem.
Create a business		Enhances your knowledge and wealth.
Join a trade association.		Increases your information and network.
Change business from non-profit to profit.		Profits create growth.
Dress to convey a positive image.		Better able to get a job, gain acceptance or advance an idea.
Pay off all credit card balances.		Eliminates interest charges.
Have no more than two credit cards.		Helps to keep credit card use under control.
Carry only cards with grace periods of 25 days or more and pay off the balance within that period.		Eliminates interest charges.
Maintain a credit score of 800 and above.		Qualifies you for the best credit.

Progress Chart Part III

Task	Date Accomplished	Benefits
Stop buying jewelry. Invest in income producing assets like stocks, bonds, property and cash.		Builds wealth.
Purchase home rather than rent.		Home appreciation, tax deduction, enhanced family stability.
Purchase only enough transportation to meet your need.		Frees up more money for college and investments.
Create a will and/ or a living trust		Protects your estate.
Maintain a healthy BMI.		Measures your health progress.
Exercise 4 to 5 times a week.		Helps you maintain the correct weight.
Stop drinking alcohol.		Makes you more alert, more sociable and saves Blacks $20 billion per year in liquor cost.
Stop gambling.		Saves $1,000 a year per person.

Progress Chart Part IV

Task	Date Accomplished	Benefits
Stop using illegal drugs.		Saves Blacks $13 billion per year. Prevents drug arrest and record.
Stop Smoking.		Saves Blacks $19 billion per year & 440 thousand US lives including 45 thousand Blacks.
Don't watch movies or TV shows that stereotype Blacks.		Black stereotyping will end.
College before the military.		Could save life and limb.
Know whom you are dating.		Eliminates surprises & reduces the divorce rate.
Do not have unprotected sex.		Can save your life.
Get married before you have children.		Unmarried women with children are a large percent of the poverty rate.
Once married, have children when you can afford to.		Enables you to pay for health, shelter & college.
Register to vote.		Protects your right to make money & escape poverty.

Appendix II – List of Jobs & Salaries

Source: U.S. Department of Labor

Job Type	Number of Jobs	Salary
Architecture and Engineering Occupations Part I Total:	2489,070	56330
Architects, Except Landscape and Naval	84980	59,590
Landscape Architects	17980	51640
Cartographers and Photogrammetrists	7810	43350
Surveyors	54650	41510
Aerospace Engineers	74380	71380
Agricultural Engineers	2550	54300
Biomedical Engineers	6960	63330
Chemical Engineers	31710	72780
Civil Engineers	205370	61000
Computer Hardware Engineers	67590	74310
Electrical Engineers	151300	68630
Electronics Engineers, Except Computer	123210	69710
Environmental Engineers	48700	62640
Health and Safety Engineers, Except Mining Safety Engineers and Inspectors	36420	59090
Industrial Engineers	151540	61940
Marine Engineers and Naval Architects	4860	66940
Materials Engineers	22920	62840
Mechanical Engineers	204310	63530
Mining and Geological Engineers, Including Mining Safety Engineers	6090	65370

Job Type	Number of Jobs	Salary
Architecture and Engineering Occupations Part II		
Nuclear Engineers	14180	80200
Petroleum Engineers	11420	81800
Architectural and Civil Drafters	99160	38580
Electrical and Electronics Drafters	39300	43200
Mechanical Drafters	69150	N/A
Aerospace Engineering and Operations Technicians	15570	51470
Civil Engineering Technicians	85920	38550
Electrical and Electronic Engineering Technicians	220800	43220
Electro-Mechanical Technicians	42130	39890
Environmental Engineering Technicians	17970	39140
Industrial Engineering Technicians	59500	43980
Mechanical Engineering Technicians	54430	42650

Job Type	Number of Jobs	Salary
Business and Financial Operations Occupations Part I Total	4676680	50580
Agents and Business Managers of Artists, Performers, and Athletes	10270	62480
Purchasing Agents and Buyers, Farm Products	17640	45130
Wholesale and Retail Buyers, Except Farm Products	131670	44200
Purchasing Agents, Except Wholesale, Retail, and Farm Products	228360	46090
Claims Adjusters, Examiners, and Investigators	200510	45350
Insurance Appraisers, Auto Damage	12110	42360
Compliance Officers, Except Agriculture, Construction, Health & Safety, & Transportation	136580	46250
Cost Estimators	188840	50450
Emergency Management Specialists	10720	45260
Employment, Recruitment, and Placement Specialists	173940	44320
Compensation, Benefits, and Job Analysis Specialists	81450	45950
Training and Development Specialists	186780	44800
Management Analysts	363890	64470
Meeting and Convention Planners	29560	39680
Accountants and Auditors	881390	50690
Appraisers and Assessors of Real Estate	59630	42420
Budget Analysts	60620	53040
Credit Analysts	66710	47170
Financial Analysts	157770	62440
Personal Financial Advisors	83820	69310

Job Type	Number of Jobs	Salary
Business and Financial Operations Occupations Part II		
Insurance Underwriters	92780	48770
Financial Examiners	24570	59860
Loan Officers	213450	50070
Tax Examiners, Collectors, and Revenue Agents	68780	45180
Tax Preparers	59520	32710

Job Type	Number of Jobs	Salary
Computer and Mathematical Occupations Total:	2825870	60350
Computer and Information Scientists, Research	25620	76970
Computer Programmers	501550	62890
Computer Software Engineers, Applications	361690	72370
Computer Software Engineers, Systems Software	261520	74490
Computer Support Specialists	493240	41920
Computer Systems Analysts	448270	63710
Database Administrators	104250	58420
Network and Computer Systems Administrators	227840	56440
Network Systems and Data Communications Analysts	126060	60300
Actuaries	13210	74720
Mathematicians	3080	73230
Operations Research Analysts	57520	59270
Statisticians	17040	57080
Mathematical Technicians	1720	44410

Job Type	Number of Jobs	Salary
Legal Occupations Total:	909379	69030
Lawyers	490000	91920
Administrative Law Judges, Adjudicators, and Hearing Officers	30520	56780
Arbitrators, Mediators, and Conciliators	5060	54340
Judges, Magistrate Judges, and Magistrates	27890	79540
Paralegals and Legal Assistants	183550	39220
Court Reporters	15300	42530
Law Clerks	40340	32280
Title Examiners, Abstractors, and Searchers	42720	35610

Job Type	Number of Jobs	Salary
Management Occupation Total:	7212360	70800
Chief Executives	455930	107670
General and Operations Managers	2064220	73570
Legislators	67400	28170
Advertising and Promotions Managers	85850	64960
Marketing Managers	189140	78410
Sales Managers	317410	77000
Public Relations Managers	64920	64280
Administrative Services Managers	311600	55460
Computer and Information Systems Managers	267310	83890
Financial Managers	570110	75430
Human Resources Managers	194470	66330
Industrial Production Managers	183050	68310
Purchasing Managers	107130	61250
Transportation, Storage, and Distribution Managers	108590	61330
Farm, Ranch, and Other Agricultural Managers	5720	46610
Construction Managers	213960	66190
Education Administrators, Preschool and Child Care Center/Program	52640	36980

Job Type	Number of Jobs	Salary
Education Administrators, Elementary and Secondary School Total	200440	71130
Education Administrators, Postsecondary	94120	66760
Engineering Managers	214760	88900
Food Service Managers	260880	38290
Funeral Directors	25300	48400
Gaming Managers	3470	59020
Lodging Managers	31040	36830
Medical and Health Services Managers	227410	64550
Natural Sciences Managers	42650	82940
Postmasters and Mail Superintendents	26640	46810
Property, Real Estate, and Community Association Managers	156180	44080
Social and Community Service Managers	100810	44540

Job Type	Number of Jobs	Salary
Life, Physical, and Social Science Occupations Total	1067730	49710
Agricultural and Food Scientists	13470	52310
Biochemists and Biophysicists	16130	61680
Microbiologists	15520	54500
Zoologists and Wildlife Biologists	12950	47400
Conservation Scientists	12750	49460
Foresters	10480	47110
Epidemiologists	3970	55590
Medical Scientists, Except Epidemiologists	46430	62650
Astronomers	900	76390
Physicists	10880	83750
Atmospheric and Space Scientists	6770	61470
Chemists	84870	55880
Materials Scientists	8360	64850
Environmental Scientists and Specialists, Including Health	57430	50700
Geoscientists, Except Hydrologists & Geographers	23030	64120
Hydrologists	7340	58570
Economists	13390	72350
Market Research Analysts	108940	58230
Survey Researchers	20690	32660
Clinical, Counseling, and School Psychologists	95640	53500
Industrial-Organizational Psychologists	1380	69950
Sociologists	1820	56560
Urban and Regional Planners	31130	50430
Anthropologists and Archeologists	4190	41800
Geographers	750	50130
Historians	2010	44850
Political Scientists	4220	78920
Agricultural and Food Science Technicians	17310	29750
Biological Technicians	43560	34030
Chemical Technicians	71000	37850
Geological and Petroleum Technicians	11930	41300
Nuclear Technicians	5230	61490
Environmental Science and Protection Technicians, Including Health	25750	36650
Forensic Science Technicians	6730	40300
Forest and Conservation Technicians	16430	32110

Job Type	Number of Jobs	Salary
Community and Social Services Occupations Total	1523890	34190
Substance Abuse and Behavioral Disorder Counselors	61580	31390
Educational, Vocational, and School Counselors	201500	45540
Marriage and Family Therapists	20380	35230
Mental Health Counselors	72590	31970
Rehabilitation Counselors	105450	28570
Child, Family, and School Social Workers	257080	35180
Medical and Public Health Social Workers	103490	38050
Mental Health and Substance Abuse Social	85550	33980
Health Educators	43890	38040
Probation Officers and Correctional Treatment Specialists	78640	41070
Social and Human Service Assistants	283060	24660
Clergy	32940	36320
Directors, Religious Activities and Education	12120	31400

Job Type	Number of Jobs	Salary
Education, Training, and Library Occupations Part I Total	7658480	39130
Business Teachers, Postsecondary	65050	59090
Computer Science Teachers, Postsecondary	29690	53790
Mathematical Science Teachers, Postsecondary	38480	53770
Architecture Teachers, Postsecondary	4960	58070
Engineering Teachers, Postsecondary	28360	69620
Agricultural Sciences Teachers, Postsecondary	11590	65410
Biological Science Teachers, Postsecondary	38580	64410
Forestry and Conservation Science Teachers, Postsecondary	1950	65170
Atmospheric, Earth, Marine, and Space Sciences Teachers, Postsecondary	7630	64210
Chemistry Teachers, Postsecondary	16610	58390
Environmental Science Teachers, Postsecondary	3630	61240
Physics Teachers, Postsecondary	11830	65050
Anthropology and Archeology Teachers, Postsecondary	4240	61230
Area, Ethnic, and Cultural Studies Teachers, Postsecondary	5070	59650
Economics Teachers, Postsecondary	11600	65620
Geography Teachers, Postsecondary	3600	58200
Political Science Teachers, Postsecondary	11230	59110
Psychology Teachers, Postsecondary	24850	57140
Sociology Teachers, Postsecondary	12890	54600
Health Specialties Teachers, Postsecondary	85220	66850
Nursing Instructors and Teachers, Postsecondary	34390	51290
Education Teachers, Postsecondary	40480	50680
Library Science Teachers, Postsecondary	4040	53520
Criminal Justice and Law Enforcement Teachers, Postsecondary	8060	47720
Law Teachers, Postsecondary	9660	79120
Social Work Teachers, Postsecondary	6250	53490

Job Type	Number of Jobs	Salary
Education, Training, and Library Occupations Part II		
Art, Drama, and Music Teachers, Postsecondary	55540	51100
Communications Teachers, Postsecondary	18100	50460
English Language and Literature Teachers, Postsecondary	51370	49770
Foreign Language and Literature Teachers, Postsecondary	18590	49130
History Teachers, Postsecondary	16710	54010
Philosophy and Religion Teachers, Postsecondary	14000	52080
Graduate Teaching Assistants	133690	24360

Job Type	Number of Jobs	Salary
Education, Training, and Library Occupations Total – Part II:		
Home Economics Teachers, Postsecondary	4350	51730
Recreation and Fitness Studies Teachers, Postsecondary	14700	44320
Vocational Education Teachers, Postsecondary	116890	41710
Preschool Teachers, Except Special Education	377540	20940
Kindergarten Teachers, Except Special Education	161610	41100
Elementary School Teachers, Except Special Education	1452160	43320
Middle School Teachers, Except Special and Vocational Education	571100	43570
Vocational Education Teachers, Middle School	18530	43340
Secondary School Teachers, Except Special and Vocational Education	980730	45370
Vocational Education Teachers, Secondary School	107680	45050
Special Education Teachers, Preschool, Kindergarten, and Elementary School	211240	44900
Special Education Teachers, Middle School	87330	43040
Special Education Teachers, Secondary School	123570	45670
Adult Literacy, Remedial Education, and GED Teachers and Instructors	58310	40230
Self-Enrichment Education Teachers	130440	32180
Archivists, Curators, and Museum Technicians	19970	38160
Librarians	150280	43750
Library Technicians	108580	25060
Audio-Visual Collections Specialists	10320	33750
Farm and Home Management Advisors	12540	41060
Instructional Coordinators	88340	48650
Teacher Assistants	1188910	19430

Job Type	Number of Jobs	Salary
Arts, Design, Entertainment, Sports, and Media Occupations Total	1508790	39770
Art Directors	20880	65570
Fine Artists, Including Painters, Sculptors, and Illustrators	9710	38330
Multi-Media Artists and Animators	30530	46700
Commercial and Industrial Designers	33600	52410
Fashion Designers	8890	56340
Floral Designers	69660	20490
Graphic Designers	136470	39670
Interior Designers	39340	43080
Merchandise Displayers and Window Trimmers	49520	24570
Set and Exhibit Designers	7840	35960
Actors	94470	36790
Producers and Directors	52130	57160
Athletes and Sports Competitors	10520	71070
Coaches and Scouts	68670	34690
Umpires, Referees, and Other Sports Officials	8750	26600
Dancers	17010	28770
Choreographers	12660	32750
Music Directors and Composers	7020	39330
Musicians and Singers	55100	46690
Announcers	50420	27590
News Analysts, Reporters and Correspondents	64130	37800
Public Relations Specialists	132390	45240
Editors	105130	44910
Technical Writers	45900	51650
Writers and Authors	40980	48120
Interpreters and Translators	18900	34680
Audio and Video Equipment Technicians	32960	35690
Broadcast Technicians	31100	33550
Radio Operators	3260	35040
Sound Engineering Technicians	9350	42300
Photographers	61250	27940
Camera Operators, Television, Video, and Motion Picture	22040	34180

Job Type	Number of Jobs	Salary
Healthcare Practitioners and Technical Occupations Part I Total	6118970	49930
Chiropractors	18060	76870
Dentists	87810	110790
Dietitians and Nutritionists	43200	41070
Optometrists	24230	87980
Pharmacists	223630	72830
Anesthesiologists	24700	131680
Family and General Practitioners	135290	110020
Internists, General	53310	126930
Obstetricians and Gynecologists	17230	133430
Pediatricians, General	24150	116550
Psychiatrists	21620	113570
Surgeons	48920	137040
Physician Assistants	56200	62410
Podiatrists	7620	94500
Registered Nurses	2217990	48240
Audiologists	11040	49700
Occupational Therapists	77080	52210
Physical Therapists	126450	59130
Radiation Therapists	13460	53480
Recreational Therapists	26830	31020
Respiratory Therapists	82930	39870
Speech-Language Pathologists	83110	50330
Veterinarians	41240	69150
Medical and Clinical Laboratory Technologists	145400	43060
Medical and Clinical Laboratory Technicians	146920	30200
Dental Hygienists	149880	56770
Cardiovascular Technologists and Technicians	40990	36510
Diagnostic Medical Sonographers	32990	48010
Nuclear Medicine Technologists	17360	51270
Radiologic Technologists and Technicians	168240	38860
Emergency Medical Technicians and Paramedics	170690	25450

Job Type	Number of Jobs	Salary
Healthcare Practitioners and Technical Occupations Part II		
Dietetic Technicians	28940	23360
Pharmacy Technicians	207140	22510
Psychiatric Technicians	59750	26920
Respiratory Therapy Technicians	28700	35220
Surgical Technologists	67460	30710
Veterinary Technologists and Technicians	51790	23620
Licensed Practical and Licensed Vocational Nurses	683790	31490
Medical Records and Health Information Technicians	142170	25370
Opticians, Dispensing	63120	28060
Orthotists and Prosthetists	4480	51510
Occupational Health and Safety Specialists and Technicians	38800	46190
Athletic Trainers	12580	35380

Acknowledgments

Special thanks to my wife Aris who did the first edit of the book.

Bibliography

Chapter 1 Black History

1) Crisis magazine Sept/Oct 2003, Single Black women and their first child.

2) Crisis magazine Sept/Oct 2003, Black children born out of wedlock.

3) US Census Bureau, Crisis magazine Sept/Oct 2003, Black children in single-mother families in 2008 living in poverty.

4) Bureau of Justice Statistics (BJS), Black male population with a police record.

Chapter 3 Black Business

1. Black Enterprise magazine, increased employment of the top 100 B.E. Industrial companies from 1998 to 2003.

2. Black Enterprise magazine, 10 BE Industrial companies with most staff from 1998 to 2009

Chapter 4 Employment and Unemployment

1. BLS National Employment Matrix

2. US Department of Labor

3. BLS Occupational Employment Statistics & Division of Occupational Outlook

Chapter 5 Income Producing Assets

1) Center for Disease Control (CDC), annual cost of alcohol, drugs and smoking.

2) National Institute on Drug Abuse (NIDA), a component of the U.S. Department of Health & Human Services, estimates cost of alcohol abuse in 1995.

Chapter 6 Communication

Black Enterprise Magazine June 2004 Issue

Chapter 8 Health & Food

1) Dietary Guidelines Advisory Committee 2000 Report, recommended calories per day.

2) Eric Topol, researcher of the Cleveland Clinic Foundation, list four classic risk factors for severe heart disease.

3) United States Department of Agriculture (USDA) -Nutrient Data Laboratory-Agricultural Research Service, list of food ingredients

4) Chowbaby.com list ingredients in fast food restaurants

5) Dietary Guidelines for Americans 2010

Chapter 9 Health & Obesity

1) Centers for Disease Control (CDC), National Center for Health Statistics (NCHS), National Health & Nutrition Examination Survey on overweight and obesity.

2) Department of Health & Human Services (HHS) and the Department of Agriculture (USDA) on healthy weight, overweight, or obese person.

Chapter 11 Family - Planning

1) US Census Bureau. Annual Social & Economic Supplement March 2008 - The Percentage of Children in Poverty.

2) National Center for Health Statistics (NCHS), Death rate from HIV.

3) Avert

Chapter 13 Crime

1) Department of Justice/BJS, rate of first incarceration by race.

2) Federal Bureau of Investigation (FBI), U.S. Census Bureau, Murder Victims by Race in 2011.

3) U.S. Census Bureau, Prisoners Under Sentence of Death in 2000.

4) US Census Bureau 2011

Chapter 14 Drinking

1) National Institute on Drug Abuse (NIDA), alcohol abuse cost.

2) National Center for Health Statistics (NCHS), Alcohol Consumption

3) Bureau of Justice Statistics (BJS), the role of Alcohol in Crime Victimization.

Chapter 15 Drugs

1) Drug Policy Alliance, drug arrest and conviction.

2) Arrestee Drug Abuse Monitoring Program 2002 (ADAM), drug use and arrest.

3) Drugnet, Drug & Alcohol Treatment & Prevention Global Network, drug treatment.

4) National Institute on Drug Abuse (NIDA), sponsored nationwide study of drug abuse treatment outcomes.

5) Drug Abuse Treatment Outcome Study (DATOS), study of drug abuse treatment outcomes.

6) Center for Substance Abuse Treatment (CSAT), support policies to enhance and expand treatment for individuals who abuse alcohol and other drugs.

7) Join Together, national resource center for communities working to reduce substance abuse and gun violence.

8) CDC

9) ADAM II Year 2008

Chapter 16 Smoking

1) American Lung Association, health dangers of smoking.

2) NCHS, CDC, National Health Interview Survey, Percentage of Current Cigarette Smoking by Adults.

Chapter 17 Military

1. U.S. Department of Justice, Bureau of Justice Statistics April 1999, Military Prison Population by Race December 31, 1996.

2. Bureau of Justice Statistics 2008

Chapter 18 Government

U.S. Census Bureau, voting in Presidential Elections.

Index

Index

Index

www.ingramcontent.com/pod-product-compliance
Lightning Source LLC
Chambersburg PA
CBHW051944280526
45789CB00009B/3164